ANGELS
of the
NORTH

NOTABLE WOMEN *of the* NORTH EAST

Joyce Quin & Moira Kilkenny

Tyne
Bridge
Publishing

Published by
Tyne Bridge Publishing 2018
City Library
Newcastle Upon Tyne
tynebridgepublishing.org.uk

ISBN: 9780951048863

Images from the collections of Newcastle Libraries
unless otherwise stated.

Layout: David Hepworth
Image research: Shawn Fairless

Contents

Preface

I moved to Northumberland in the late 1980s and was immediately attracted to the area, to the landscape – the wild open countryside and its industrial heritage - but perhaps most of all to the people.

This book celebrates the contribution that the women of the North East have made, locally, nationally and internationally. Some of the women featured are very well known, lodged firmly in the national consciousness. The heroine Grace Darling became an overnight sensation thanks to coverage in the national press; it became, perhaps, the first example of media frenzy. *The Times* wrote effusively, 'Is there in the whole field of history, or of fiction, even one instance of female heroism to compare with this?'

In the year that marks the 100-year anniversary of the Representation of the People Act, giving (some) women the right to vote, it's heartening that so many North Eastern women played pivotal roles in that struggle, often at great personal sacrifice. Kathleen Brown was imprisoned three times because of her civil disruption and of course Emily Wilding Davison gave her life. North Eastern campaigners like Josephine Butler, Emily Davies, Charlotte Marsh and Connie Lewcock made a huge contribution to highlight the rights of women, fundamentally changing the attitude of society, politicians and government.

2018 marks one-hundred years since the end of the First World War. That conflict catapulted women into roles that were left by men who had gone to fight. They became railway guards and ticket collectors, bus and tram conductors, post office workers, police officers, firefighters and bank cashiers. However, they received lower wages for doing the same work and that began some of the earliest demands for equal pay. Again, another northern heroine was a leader in that campaigning: engineer Rachel Parsons, who in 1920 set up an all-female engineering company!

I'm delighted that many of the chosen North East heroines are writers. Catherine Cookson and Denise Roberston wrote exciting, accessible and immensely popular books – like my *Vera* novels, their stories feature strong, female characters – often putting modest, working class women centre stage. The North East has produced many female writers. Perhaps one of the most interesting is Mary Astell. Many cite Mary Wollstonecraft's *A Vindication of the Rights of Woman* published in 1790 as the first feminist book, but Newcastle's Astell predates that and the first wave of feminism by nearly a century with *A Serious Proposal to the Ladies for the Advancement of their True and Greatest Interest* (1694) and later *Some Reflections upon Marriage* (1700) in which she highlights the inequality in marriage and the dependency of women on their husbands for their legal, social, and financial status.

None of the women profiled in this book, which spans 1580 to 2016, are alive today, but women of the North East continue to make a strong, lasting and significant contribution. Sunderland gave us journalist Kate Adie and musician Lauren Laverne who is currently curating the Great Exhibition of the North. Steph McGovern from Middlesbrough appears on television holding businesses and politicians to account. We're doing well in the world of sport – Hartlepool's Savannah Marshall was the first ever women's boxing world champion in 2012, later winning a Commonwealth gold medal. Lucy Bronze from Alnwick played in the England team for the Women's World Cup in 2015, and wheelchair racer turned politician, Tanni Grey-Thompson is Chancellor of Northumbria University. We have many female business leaders, innovators and entrepreneurs, and three of the North East's major local authorities have female chief executives.

Women may not have smashed through the glass ceiling yet, but because of the effort, dedication and determination of the women of the North East, the cracks are beginning to show.

Ann Cleeves, North Tyneside, 2018

Introduction

This year, 2018, has marked the centenary of the year when some women in Britain were allowed to vote for the first time. It has also been the year of the 'Great Exhibition of the North' when we have been reflecting on the North's past successes, drawing on these for further inspiration and aiming to encourage the aspirations of our young people, girls and boys. For these reasons it seemed to us to be a highly appropriate time for a book on the achievements of North East women of the past.

We are not only joint authors of this book but we are also friends and neighbours and the idea for the book arose from a conversation we had while at a party in our local village! In discovering our joint interest in North East history and heritage we were talking about some of the books which had been written about the North East's most famous sons - books such as Richard Welford's classic *Men of Mark 'Twixt Tyne and Tweed* or Lawson's *Tyneside Celebrities*. But, we asked each other, where are the books on the North East's eminent women?

In *Angels of the North* we have chosen forty women who are either from the North East - or have strong connections to it - to highlight. Some of these women are household names whereas others have significant achievements to their credit but are in danger of being forgotten. All of them - we felt - were women to be proud of. We wanted to pay tribute to them and to celebrate their lives and their work.

This book is really just a beginning. There are of course many other women of the North East we could have written about and who deserve to be commemorated and celebrated. In the artistic world alone we could mention Laura Gladstone Adams, Sophia Atkinson, Margaret Wrightson and Millicent Sowerby. We have also restricted ourselves to women of the past rather than notable women of today who are still making their mark. Furthermore we have found, in the course of our writing, that there is much unpublished material about some of our subjects which it would be wonderful to make publicly available. For researchers and scholars there is a great deal to investigate further and to write about and indeed several excellent PhD theses remain to be written exploring aspects of the ideas and lives of these eminent women!

Although we have each written separate profiles about individual women we have been struck by the number of times the lives of our subjects have criss-crossed and how many of them knew each other. Of course this is not surprising in the case of the North East's many eminent suffragettes who, it is clear, were bound together in friendship and solidarity. However other instances were serendipitous discoveries as we researched our subjects' histories. Marion Phillips and Ethel Williams both worked as co-investigators on the Poor Law Commission set up by Sidney and Beatrice Webb. Margaret Bondfield arranged London accommodation for suffragette Connie Lewcock. Emily Davies and Josephine Butler had met each other but had different ideas about how best to pursue the goal of women's access to higher education - particularly in Cambridge. Ellen Wilkinson and her political adversary Irene Ward were friends. Irene Ward always stoutly defended the reputation of her election opponent Margaret Bondfield. One of Ruth Dodds' early and memorable experiences of speaking in public occurred when she had to substitute at short notice for Ethel Williams. Despite their age difference Elizabeth Montagu met and corresponded with the young Mary Bowes commending her scholarship and encouraging her literary ambitions. There was also a strong connection between Elizabeth Elstob and Mary Astell, both Novocastrians. Elizabeth became part of the literary group around Mary Astell, the same group which raised money for the publication of Elstob's *Anglo-Saxon Grammar*.

As we have noted this is an appropriate, and perhaps even a crucial, time to trumpet the North and the North East's achievements. Northerners have a natural tendency to view self-publicity with suspicion and are not given to boasting - it is not a regional trait. It is true, too, that in an England, and a UK, dominated by London-based media our achievements and activities often seem to get overlooked. In that sense we hope that our book can be a timely wake-up call as well as a celebration and heartfelt tribute to some of our country's most remarkable and truly inspiring women.

Joyce Quin and Moira Kilkenny

A Serious
PROPOSAL
TO THE
LADIES,
FOR THE
Advancement of their
True and Greateſt
INTEREST.

PART I.

By a Lover of her SEX.

The Third Edition Corrected.

LONDON,
Printed by *T. W.* for *R. Wilkin,* at
the *King's-Head* in St. *Paul's*
Church-Yard, 1 6 9 6.

Mary Astell (1666-1731)

Pioneer Feminist Writer

If all Men are born free, how is it that all Women are born Slaves?

Born in Newcastle, Mary was the first major feminist writer in the English language. She coined the phrase, 'If All Men are born free, how is it that all Women are born slaves?' (*Reflections on Marriage*. 1700) Mary rose to become a controversial figure and a shining light of London's early eighteenth century intelligentsia.

Mary Astell was born in 1666 to Peter and Mary (Errington) Astell. Her father was a wealthy coal merchant, an Anglican and a Royalist. Mary was baptised at St. John's Church and lived on Tyneside throughout her early life. As we know, girls then were lucky if they received any education at all and then it was just enough to make them marriageable. However Mary was fortunate and for several years was educated in Latin, French, logic and natural philosophy by her uncle, Ralph Astell, a man of letters. Mary was a precocious and ardent pupil. After her uncle's death she continued to read widely. She was mainly influenced by the Cambridge followers of Plato, who emphasised rationality and an ascetic disciplined life. Her social and political views were shaped by the Tory Royalist views of her family and she herself became a devout Anglican.

Mary was twelve when her father died, leaving the family in such poverty, that Mary and her mother had to live with an aunt in order to finance her younger brother Peter's higher education. There was no dowry for Mary!

Ten years later Mary was orphaned and went to London to try to earn a living as a writer. This was a bold enterprise given the almost complete absence of any published work by women at that time, except for the playwright, Aphra Benn. Mary was greatly assisted in London by the Archbishop of Canterbury, William Sancroft, to whom she had written for help. He gave her both financial assistance and some life-changing introductions to a circle of aristocratic, intellectual and influential women who were to become her disciples as well as her patrons. He also introduced her to her future publisher, the London bookseller, Richard Wilkin. Mary settled in Chelsea but remained dependent on the financial support of her patrons and friends. These included, Lady Ann Coventry, Lady Elizabeth Hastings, Lady Catherine Jones, Viscountess

Ranleigh, Lady Mary Chudleigh, and Elizabeth Elstob, a fellow Novocastrian.

Mary's biggest idea was that women were just as rational as men and just as deserving of education. This contradicted the prevailing view that women were innately inferior to men. Influential philosophers such as Jean Jacques Rousseau, saw femaleness as a form of arrested development, a condition somewhere between childhood and manhood, so they believed that women required the *protection* of men. Mary however argued that women were the equals of men with the same intellectual capacity, the real problem was that eighteenth century society deprived women of the same educational opportunities as men. She was the first woman to expound these ideas that were centuries ahead of her time, and expressed them in her first publication, *A Serious Proposal to the Ladies for the Advancement of their True and Greatest Interest* (1694). She urged women to aspire to a life of the mind, saying that education was more satisfying than the passing fads of fashion and social advancement. She addressed women directly, asking them how could they be content to be in the world, 'like tulips in a garden to make a fine show and be good for nothing?' She urged women to reject marriages where the husband was a tyrant. The controversial issues raised, together with the rational and polished style of this, her first piece of feminist writing, established her reputation as a writer and a logician and the work was widely read and hotly debated.

In 1697, she issued Part 2 of a *A Serious Proposal*, in which she suggested the establishment of a female college, a place of retreat where women could study and enjoy each other's company, where they could learn to value and train their minds, a haven for women who did not marry or a temporary retreat for women who would eventually marry. (Girton College Cambridge, the first women's college, was not established until 1869, nearly two hundred years later.) In May and September 1709, the popular *Tatler* Magazine, included cruelly satirical articles by Jonathan Swift and Richard Steele about her ideas. She was dubbed 'Madonella' and the imagined inmates of her proposed college were scathingly described as the Order of Platonics, cowering nuns hiding from the real world. Daniel Defoe published his criticisms of the Proposal for an all-female college but then went on to suggest a similar idea himself.

Astell's third feminist work was *Some Reflections upon Marriage* (1700). In it she describes the utter dependency of women on their husbands for their legal, social, and financial status. Her argument is that since marriage in a patriarchal society subjects women to the absolute authority of frequently unjust or abusive husbands, they would be better off avoiding marriage altogether! Under these circumstances women should educate themselves, seek other ways to support themselves and cultivate friendships rather than marry. She writes: 'If a Woman can neither Love nor Honour, she does ill in promising to obey.' We can only imagine the range of responses these radical descriptions of women's social and intellectual positions provoked.

Mary Astell also engaged effectively in the political, religious and philosophical debates of the day. She corresponded with John Locke and in 1695 she published her philosophical letters to the Cambridge scholar, John Norris, on the Love of God. In 1704 she wrote three treatises espousing the cause of the Stuarts and the High Church and *The Christian Religion, As professed by a Daughter of the Church of England*. In this work she wondered why God had given women the power to reason if they were not allowed to use it.

Mary Astell's works were very widely read and went into many editions, but she was never part of the establishment because of her views on women. All her works were published either anonymously or under a pseudonym and although driven to write to try and encourage a more enlightened approach to women she tried to avoid the limelight because she disliked publicity and found it very stressful. For whatever reason, maybe to prove her point about women's intellectual abilities, perhaps because she ran out of courage, in 1709, she retired from public life and opened charity school for girls in Chelsea, which she had established, finding the site, raising the funds and devising the curriculum.1709 was the same year *The Tatler* had lampooned her ideas so cruelly.

When she was 60, Mary accepted an invitation to live with Lady Catherine Jones, the renowned chemist and sister of Robert Boyle and one of Mary's circle of intellectual women friends. She remained there until her death from cancer in May 1731. She was sixty-five. She was buried in the churchyard of All Saints, in Chelsea.

Logic and reason, the great tools of the Enlightenment, were Mary Astell's passion, and she was the first to bring them to the debate about women. She was an inspiration to other eighteenth century writers and thinkers, men and women, Daniel Defoe, Lady Mary Chudleigh, Lady Mary W. Montagu, Lady Catherine Jones, Samuel Johnson and Mary Wollstonecraft, to name a few. Furthermore, as one of the very earliest English authors in the age of mass distribution, her feminist analysis of the condition of women in the eighteenth century provided the foundation for the modern women's movement and has served as a powerful role model for campaigners down the ages. In short Mary Astell should be celebrated and remembered as a powerful force in the eighteenth century Enlightenment and as the first English feminist.

The exact site of Mary Astell's grave in All Saints Churchyard, Chelsea, is unknown. The only plaque in her memory is inside the Church of All Saints, Chelsea.

Gertrude Margaret Lowthian Bell CBE (1868-1926)

Explorer, Archeologist, Arab diplomat and Scholar

A commemorative plaque at Washington Hall records, 'Gertrude Bell: Scholar, Historian, Distinguished servant of the State: Born here, 14th July 1868, died Baghdad, 12th July 1926.'

Gertrude Bell was certainly one of the most remarkable women of modern times. The daughter of Sir Hugh Lowthian Bell, the wealthy enlightened colliery owner and iron master of Middlesbrough, Gertrude's early years were spent between the family homes, Rounton Grange near Northallerton, a beautiful Arts and Crafts house, and their London Residence in Sloane Street. Throughout her life, Gertrude enjoyed a close and loving relationship with her father and stepmother, Lady Frances (Olliffe) Bell, an author and playwright herself. Gertrude's own mother died when Gertrude was three years old. Both parents fostered her independent character as well as her love of learning. 'Dearest Papa,' encouraged and financed her education, her extensive travel and archaeological excavations.

From the outset, Gertrude was a girl of outstanding mental and physical attributes. Exceptionally, she read History at Lady Margaret Hall, Oxford and in 1888 became the first woman to qualify for a First in Modern History. Women then were barely tolerated in academic life, and were not allowed to receive their degrees at a graduation ceremony!

A brilliant scholar and gifted writer, during the course of her life Gertrude

Left) A young Gertrude Bell. Below) A group including Winston Churchill, Gertrude Bell (centre) and T.E. Lawrence on camels in front of the Sphinx during the Cairo conference, 1921.

became a remarkable linguist speaking eight languages including fluent Arabic.

Before outlining the pioneering achievements for which Gertrude is remarkable, it should be noted that she was not entirely a 'modern' woman, for she opposed women's suffrage and was a founder member of the Northern Branch of the Women's National Anti-Suffrage League.

Gertrude was opinionated and strong willed. An attractive auburn haired young woman with a life-long love of beautiful clothes and the finances to indulge in them, she was duly presented at Court. However the scholar in her was stronger than the debutante, and she chose exploration and travel rather than London high society, this at a time when most women never set foot on foreign soil unless they emigrated!

Her passion for the history and culture of Arab peoples began in earnest with her first visit to Persia in 1892, when she was twenty-four. While staying with her uncle, Sir Frank Lascelles, British Minister in Teheran, she described Teheran as the Garden of Eden, the epitome of the living East. This was when Gertrude began to express herself in the series of letters she wrote to her family over the next thirty-four years and for which she is famous. The letters indicate her deep love of Arabia and its people. They were edited by her stepmother and have never been out of print since 1927.

Tehran was also where she met and fell in love with Henry Cadogan, secretary at the British Embassy. They were briefly engaged, but when it emerged that he could not support a household her father advised her to return home and the relationship was ended. She later wrote that this engagement had promised her her one supreme chance of happiness.

After the desolation of this broken engagement, Gertrude threw herself into a frenzied schedule of travel throughout Europe and, between 1901 and 1903, she added mountaineering to her activities. She conquered both La Meije and Mont Blanc, and the 'Gertrudspitze,' in the Bernese Oberland is named after her because she was the first to cross it.

However, it was to Arabia that she was drawn and it was there that she accomplished her extraordinary life's work. Between 1903 and 1913 Gertrude Bell undertook four major expeditions to the desert lands of the Middle East, often travelling in uncharted territories, across inhospitable terrain in extreme climatic conditions. She visited and discovered vanished civilisations, studied Arab culture and Arab tribes and photographed and recorded all that she could. In the process she worked hard to become fluent in Arabic, for as she wrote she wanted *real* knowledge of the tribes, 'to get deep into the gossip of the East'. She travelled with her male servant, Fattuh, an Armenian Christian, and an army of bearers. She took a tent, bed, table and chairs and all necessary equipment, as well as a library and notebooks, sometimes a theodolite and always her photographic equipment. She also took an expensive wardrobe and fine crockery. Bell acquired all the skills of archaeologists, she even trained with the Royal Geographic Society in surveying techniques.

In 1900, using Jerusalem as a base, she explored as many Ancient sites in Syria and Jordan as she could. She travelled south to the fabulous ruins of Petra, north to Damascus and finally northwest to the ancient ruins of Palmyra, all the while speaking Arabic. She travelled freely among the Bedouin in Jordan and camped among the Bika Arabs at Pisgah. Her careful documentation of this trip, including more than 500 photographs, today forms part of an internationally valued archive. In 1907 she summarised this work in *Syria: The Desert and the Sown*. Gertrude made her name as a writer through her many such writings, as well as a fine translation of the poetry of the Persian poet, Hafiz.

Gertrude, a passionate young woman, had another tortured love affair, this time with a married man, Charles Doughtie-Wylie. Things came to a head in March 1914 when he asked if she would be content to be his mistress and although she refused, they continued to correspond. In January 1915 they were able to meet and spend four days alone together, however soon after he was sent to join the expeditionary force to storm Gallipoli and tragically was killed in April 1915.

In 1913, while she was suffering in her personal life, Gertrude undertook her final and greatest desert expedition to Hayil, capital of the Nejd, down in the centre of Arabia. This, involved organising enormous supplies, provisions, gifts, equipment, the training of staff and the purchase of seventeen transport camels. Over four gruelling months she travelled 1,500 miles, from Damascus to Hayil. She mapped as much as she could and gathered a great deal of intelligence. The journey was full of anxiety because there was inter-tribal fighting going on all around. She wrote, 'murder is as common as spilling milk.' When she reached Hayil she was detained for eleven days and then inexplicably released. On the return journey she travelled east to Baghdad and arrived there utterly exhausted. By May she was back in Damascus and then returned to England and her beloved home at Rounton Grange.

The outbreak of war in 1914 led to huge changes in Gertrude's life and she was summoned to work for British Intelligence in the Arab Bureau in Cairo dealing with Middle Eastern affairs. T.E. Lawrence (Lawrence of Arabia) also worked there, 'beloved boy' she called him. She was the only woman to hold official positions in the Arab Bureau and when, in April 1917, Britain defeated the Turks and occupied Baghdad, she went there to join the new British administration under Sir Percy Cox, as his Oriental Secretary. British policy was to ensure that the Arabs supported the British Government in its efforts to defeat the Ottoman Empire in return for British support for an independent Arab State. So when, with British encouragement, the Arab revolt began in 1916, her unique knowledge of desert tribes, the trust the Arabs had in her and the intelligence she had garnered on her great desert journeys, particularly on the 1913 expedition, meant that her services were of the utmost importance. General Sir Gilbert Clayton wrote, 'I attribute much of the success of Colonel Lawrence's enterprises to 'Intelligence', in which Miss Bell had a very large part.'

Gertrude Bell had become, in effect, head of the Iraq branch of the Arab Bureau, and Official Correspondent to Cairo. Her work led to two major awards, in October 1917 she received the CBE for her war work and in 1918 she received the Royal Geographic Society Founder's Medal, 'For her important explorations and travels in Asia Minor, Syria, Arabia and on the Euphrates.'

After all the years of study, preparation and hardship she had finally come into her own, she had risen to the very top and had become virtually indispensable in a man's world. She said she could not have expected a better destiny.

In 1919 she attended the Paris Peace Conference as the representative of the Arab Bureau and in 1921 attended the Cairo Conference. She was instrumental in the selection of Prince Faisal as the new King of Mesopotamia, Iraq, and most famously she was central in drawing the borders of Iraq. She wrote to her father in December 1921, 'I had a well spent morning at the office making out the Southern Desert frontier of Iraq ... One way and another, I think I have succeeded in compiling a reasonable frontier.'

Although by this time the strain of the past few years had begun to take its toll on Gertrude's health, one final task awaited her. She established the Iraq Museum of Antiquities, opened by King Faisal in June 1926, but only one month later she died suddenly. The cause of death was an overdose of sleeping pills, whether this was an accident or deliberate has never been established.

Gertrude Bell's loss to the Arabs whom she loved so dearly is best expressed in the inscription dedicated to her in the museum. A fitting epitaph to a great lady, it reads:

'GERTRUDE BELL, Whose memory the Arabs will ever hold in reverence and affection created this Museum in 1923 being their Honorary Director of Antiquities for Iraq. With wonderful knowledge and devotion, she assembled the most precious objects in it and through the heat of the summer worked on them until the day of her death on 12 July 1926'.

Margaret Bondfield (1873-1953)

The First Woman Cabinet Minister

Margaret Bondfield, MP for Wallsend.

'The best man of the lot' (Bernard Shaw)

The above quotation would make most of today's women MPs or candidates wince. Yet at the time it was a handsome compliment given that when it was uttered not all women had the vote and there were only three women MPs! Indeed, Margaret Bondfield's achievements are astounding. She was the first woman to chair the TUC, the first Woman Privy Councillor, the first woman Junior Minister and then the first Woman Cabinet Minister. And at the zenith of this stellar career - from 1926-1931 - she was the Member of Parliament for Wallsend.

It is surprising how little has been written about her. No full biography about her exists although she published her autobiography *A Life's Work* in 1948 when she was seventy-eight. Otherwise she is a largely forgotten pioneer of the British Labour movement. Perhaps the reason for this is that she was tarnished by being part of Ramsay MacDonald's 1929 Labour Government and was even suspected by some of being prepared to follow him and his colleagues into splitting from the Labour Party and forming the National Coalition in 1931. However, suspicions of treachery are hard to justify. While Margaret had a record of being prepared to compromise with political opponents in order (as she argued) to try to make some progress rather than none, her loyalty to both the Trade Union movement and the Labour Party stood the test of many years and was a lifelong commitment. She may have made misjudgements in trying to mitigate policies rather than opposing them but her commitment to do what she could to move towards a fairer society was genuine and sincere. After 1931 she stayed in the Labour Party, strongly supported Clement Attlee as Party Leader, sought to stand again for Parliament for Labour and undertook many speaking engagements for the Labour Party and her Union. She continued to campaign for women's rights and workers' rights until the end of her life.

Margaret's childhood was spent in Chard, Somerset, where she was the tenth child in a family of eleven. Times were tough, particularly after her father lost his job as a skilled artisan lace maker when the firm he worked for closed down and he was forced to get what other work he could. The family grew many of their own vegetables and, in contrast to the cases of abject poverty in her neighbourhood, Margaret was aware that they were still - just - able to make ends meet. Her father was a keen Congregationalist and in common with many non-conformists of the age was convinced of the importance of education and of self-improvement. Margaret was educated at Chard elementary school and became a pupil-teacher there under a temporary posting at the age of thirteen.

A significant and, as it would turn out, life-changing event occurred when her school position was abolished - a qualified teacher taking it over as a full-time role - and Margaret went to Brighton to become a shop assistant. She became interested in the working conditions of shop girls, an interest which intensified when, a couple of years later, she went to work in London and witnessed some of the appalling conditions they endured. She particularly detested the living-in system whereby shop girls were given low wages for long working hours and were confined to cramped living quarters with inadequate, poor quality meals. The girls were not allowed out without permission and usually had little privacy in their dingy, badly ventilated dormitories. Margaret joined the Shop Assistants' Union, started campaigning and became more and more committed. She wrote articles for the Union newspaper and took part in the inquiry into working conditions in London shops launched by the Women's Industrial Council. Her report, completed in 1898, brought to public attention the iniquities of the 'living-in' system and was not only publicised widely but led to the Shop Assistants' Act, passed to tackle some of the worst injustices the shop girls faced.

Margaret, remarkably, was the only woman delegate from any union to the TUC Conference in 1899 and for the next ten years or so she fulfilled the role of Assistant Secretary of the Shop Assistants' Union. Trade Unionism and left-wing politics went hand in hand and Margaret also became active in the Labour Representation Committee, then the Independent Labour Party and in this way was influential in the establishment of the Labour Party itself. She worked with other pioneering women including Margaret Gladstone, the wife of Ramsay MacDonald and with Mary MacArthur, her close friend in the Women's Trade Union League. It was with Mary MacArthur that she founded the National Federation of Women Workers.

Margaret was also active in the suffrage movement and in the Adult Suffrage Society, but, although supporting the cause of votes for women, she was clear that what she wanted to see above all was universal suffrage for men and women without any additional age or property qualification. She expressed this view forcefully when in 1918, at the end of the First World War, women were at last given the vote, but only women who were over thirty and who met the necessary property-related requirement.

Through all her activities Margaret became well-known nationally and was highly respected for her abilities as a public speaker and as a powerful advocate for the causes she promoted. Even without her subsequent political career she has a good claim to be regarded as one of the most influential women in public life in the late nineteenth and early twentieth centuries.

Margaret was elected MP for Northampton in 1923 after two unsuccessful attempts. She rapidly became an active participant in the House of Commons, highlighting injustices and speaking up for measures to encourage the employment of women and an improvement in their working conditions. She was also quickly promoted when Labour took office in 1924, becoming a Minister in the Ministry of Labour - a difficult task when unemployment was already rife, although she did introduce measures such as greater assistance to the worst off and a substantial programme of relief work. Government office was short-lived however, as the Labour government was defeated in the 1924 election and Margaret herself lost her seat.

Margaret's colleagues and good friends among the Labour leadership - such as Arthur Henderson, MP for Newcastle East - were keen to see her return to Parliament and encouraged her to stand for selection in Wallsend where a bye-election was to be held. She was duly selected, with strong trade union support, and was then elected with a majority of 9,000. It was reported that 'women danced in the street, men broke into song, and a general chant of 'Maggie MP' was heard. A special victory cake was baked for her by her jubilant women supporters.

Once again, the euphoria of victory was short-lived as Margaret was appointed to the Conservative Government's all-party parliamentary 'Blanesburgh' Committee, which had a remit to look at unemployment benefit. While she clearly did not agree with all the Committee's recommendations, she put her name to the report because it had at least recommended unlimited unemployment benefit for the first time. However, unsurprisingly, that did not appease her critics, both in Wallsend and nationally, who were aghast at another principal recommendation of the report concerning the need to 'be genuinely seeking work'. In areas of mass unemployment, fears that such a provision would be implemented over-strictly (which sadly turned out to be the case) were widespread. Because of this, Margaret, although vigorously defending her position, was opposed in the 1929 election in Wallsend by candidates from the left and right, but was nonetheless re-elected with an increased majority.

Labour's second government was a minority government, taking office at a time of severe worldwide economic slump. Margaret became the first Woman Cabinet Minister when she was appointed Minister for Labour. Her junior Minister, whom she admired, was Jack Lawson, a North Eastern colleague and MP for Chester-le-Street. The challenges she faced were colossal. She did abolish the hated 'genuinely seeking work' provision and managed, initially, to introduce some increases in unemployment rates. However the reduction in available government funds because of the economic recession caused huge difficulties. Subsequent action by the government to cut the cost of benefits by targeting married women in particular gained her and her colleagues much opprobrium. Ramsay MacDonald's decision to head a 'national' coalition government was, however, a step too far for Margaret, who opted to stay with the Labour Party under Arthur Henderson and to go into Opposition. Along with most Labour MPs, she lost her seat in the 1931 election and again, like many colleagues, failed to be re-elected in 1935. Her ambition to return to Parliament after that was thwarted by the postponement of elections during the Second World War, by which time she was sixty-seven years of age.

After retiring from her full-time trade union post in 1938, Margaret continued to champion Trade Unionism both at home and, importantly, abroad. She had first become involved in the International Labour Organisation in the 1920s and served on its Overseas Development Committee for most of that decade. In the 1930s she continued to be active in fostering international trade union links in many countries and helped consolidate women's trade unionism, particularly in the United States and Canada. She had also made many friends in Russia despite her increasing distrust of and opposition to Soviet Communism.

To the end of her life she kept up many friendships, personal and political, as well as remaining close to her brother Frank. Throughout her life, her Congregational, non-conformist Christianity remained important and continued to inspire her.

There is no doubt that she was a remarkable woman. She combined a capacity for hard work with resilience, dedication and fierce loyalty to friends and colleagues. Even those who disagreed with the causes and policies she espoused paid tribute to her sincerity and her courage when faced with public hostility. Her work and achievements were recognised with the award of the Companion of Honour and an honorary degree from the University of Bristol. She was also made a Freeman of the Borough of Chard, the town of her childhood.

To the quotation of Bernard Shaw alluded to earlier might be added another from Sybil Thorndike, the renowned actress, who said 'whatever party Margaret Bondfield belongs to I shall unhesitatingly vote for her - as I believe she is the sort of woman who ought to have a hand in the affairs of this country'.

Margaret Bondfield died in 1953 at the age of eighty. Clement Attlee gave the address at her funeral. There seem to be no memorials or plaques to her memory in the North East but the North Tyneside Fabian Society produced a booklet commemorating her achievements (and those of Grace Colman) in 1995. There is a plaque commemorating Margaret in the Guildhall in Chard - coincidentally unveiled by Barbara Castle who had refused to pay tribute to Margaret, because of her closeness to Ramsay MacDonald, in North Tyneside's booklet. The plaque reads 'she devoted her life to improving the lot of the downtrodden'. Chard also has a street named after her, there is a Bondfield hall of residence in Northampton University and there is a Margaret Bondfield nursery school in Greenwich.

Mary Eleanor Bowes, by J.C. Dillman, 1800. (Bowes Museum)

Mary Eleanor Bowes
Countess of Strathmore and Kinghorne
(1749-1800)

Tragic Heiress

The Countess described the events of her life as 'so uncommon as to stagger the belief of Posterity.' Fifty years later when Thackeray published his first novel, *The Luck of Barry Lyndon*, based on Mary's life and telling the tale of the brutish Irish adventurer outwitted by the rich heiress he had tricked into marriage, many critics thought the story just too outlandish to be credible!

Mary's childhood was idyllic. She was brought up in luxury, the only child of George Bowes the wealthy coal magnate and owner of the Gibside estate in County Durham. The enormous wealth of the family, built on the coal seams beneath their estates, can be gauged by the great mansion Bowes built on the banks of the Derwent, the beautiful Palladian chapel, the column to British Liberty, the orangery constructed to encourage his daughter's love of plants and the Great Walk along which he raced his horses. Today the property is owned by the National Trust.

Mary's father doted on her and ensured she enjoyed a wide and thorough education. She was an intelligent girl with a gift for languages and a love of botany. Even as a child Mary's accomplishments brought her to the attention of Elizabeth Montagu, founder of the intellectual Blue-Stocking Club. Father and daughter were very close and her father's death, when she was only eleven, was an emotional catastrophe for her. For the rest of her life she was searching for an equally stimulating male companion. She did inherit his vast fortune and became the richest heiress in the kingdom and, as such, the subject of many marriage proposals. Her choice of husband at the age of eighteen, was the very handsome John Lyon, ninth Earl of Strathmore and Kinghorne.

By the terms of the marriage Mary's husband had to take the name of Bowes. The Strathmore family name Lyon, was later changed to Bowes-Lyon. Mary Eleanor Bowes was the great, great, great, great grandmother of the Queen.

The marriage was not happy, the Earl was an honest if dull gentleman whereas she was rather lively, spoilt and with serious intellectual interests, not ready to settle down to a quiet life on his Scottish estates. In 1776 she published a play in blank verse, *The Siege of Jerusalem*. Although discouraged by her husband, she pursued her interest in botany. The marriage did produce five children in only six years. Tragically, Lord Strathmore developed tuberculosis and died in 1776 on board a ship bound for Lisbon in search of a cure.

Mary had been having an affair with one George Grey for some time prior to her husband's death and had endured three abortions. When she found herself carrying his child for a fourth time she reluctantly became engaged to him. But then, only months after being widowed, she met the Irishman, Andrew Robinson Stoney, a widowed lieutenant on half pay in the 30th Regiment. He was an imposing, attractive, charming fortune-hunter, a man with a vicious and calculating disposition. Undeterred by tales of his ill treatment of his first wife, she allowed herself to be tricked into marrying him. Stoney, as he was known, went to great lengths to arrange a phoney duel, which he said he had fought in defence of Mary's honour. Feigning a mortal wound, he begged her, 'a dying man's last wish,' to marry him and she agreed. They were married in January 1777 amidst a blaze of publicity and even though doctors had sworn his wounds were fatal, Mary's new husband made a miraculous (disastrous) recovery!

In the summer of 1777 Mary gave birth to a daughter, Mary, the child of George Grey. Later she and her husband had a son, William, but by then the marriage was a disaster. Soon after the marriage, Bowes discovered the Prenuptial Trust Mary had signed to prevent him from controlling her fortune. She had done this because in the eighteenth century a married women could not normally keep her own property, it automatically passed to her husband. Since Bowes had married her for her fortune, he was incandescent with rage and forced her to revoke it. Control of the fortune and the family then passed to him and for the next eight years he wreaked his revenge upon his wife. He beat her, starved her, abused her and kept her prisoner, he also prevented her from seeing her children. After only one year of marriage, having beaten her into submission, he forced Mary to write her now famous, Confessions of the Countess of Strathmore, a list of her past crimes and indiscretions, in return for which he promised to stop beating her! Then in 1793 he published and publicised them and used them against her in the law suits that followed. She of course subsequently denied their veracity as they had been written under duress.

Eventually in 1785, with the help of her servants, particularly Mary Morgan who became her lifelong friend, Lady Mary managed to escape and took lodgings in Holborn, under the name of Mrs Jeffries. In fear of her life she took the desperate and brave decision to raise an action for divorce through the Church courts. There was no civil divorce court and no divorce law in England until 1857. The only avenue open to her was through the ecclesiastical London Consistory Court, which could decree that a couple should live separately when one was at risk from the other. Although this was a lengthy and expensive process and Mary was penniless, she did have friends and servants willing to lend her money. In May 1786 she was granted a divorce on the grounds of her husband's cruelty and adultery. Totally unbowed, Bowes initiated two appeals against the decision, both went against him and the divorce was finally ratified in 1789.

Meanwhile, in November 1786, having discovered Mary's whereabouts, Bowes kidnapped her and carried her off to Durham to try to force her to withdraw her divorce plea. After an eight-day trauma and a dramatic chase around the countryside, Mary, bruised and bleeding, dressed in rags and freezing cold, was freed and criminal proceedings were immediately begun against her husband. In May 1787, he was found guilty, imprisoned for three years and bound over for a further fourteen years.

In the eighteenth century married women had no legal standing at all and when women married they became their husband's property. They, as well as their property and any children, passed entirely into the husband's control. This remained the case until The Married Women's Property Act of 1882. Despite her own total lack of legal standing, Mary decided to lodge an appeal in the name of one of her male trustees, to have the deed by which her wealth had been transferred to Bowes set aside, and the prenuptial deed of January 1777 restored. She was still without money, unable to pay her legal costs unless she won the case and aware that once again every detail of her married life would be exposed in the press. She persisted and her gamble paid off, she won! The jury found in her favour, this was ratified in the Court of Chancery and the vast wealth she had inherited from her father was restored to her after twelve bitter years. It is hard to imagine the relief she must have felt after all the suffering her foolish marriage had brought upon her.

Bowes was now deprived of all money and property, his marriage to Mary was dissolved and he spent the rest of his life in prison.

Mary initiated one further legal action and in 1790 Bowes was forced to restore the two youngest children, Mary and William to their mother. This was another considerable legal victory, for at the time it was almost unheard of for even the most debauched of fathers to lose custody of their children.

Free from her cruel husband, reunited with her children and with her fortune restored, the Countess transferred the title and estates to her eldest son John, in exchange for a modest annual pension that allowed her respite and rest after her ordeals. She was forty-one years old.

For the next ten years Lady Mary lived in quiet retirement in Hampshire. In 1795 she wrote a 300-page narrative, describing in harrowing detail the atrocities she had suffered at the hands of her second husband. Lady Mary died five years later at Christchurch, Hampshire in April 1800 and is buried in the south cross of Westminster Abbey.

Gibside in County Durham, home of the Bowes family.

Lady Mary's life was both tragic and heroic. Wickedness and weakness combined to ensure that she did not fulfil her literary or scientific ambitions, though her lifelong love of learning did sustain her through difficult times. Instead her bravery in initiating three successful lawsuits at a time when the law of the land counted married women as mere chattels provided inspiration for hundreds of other women trapped in bad marriages. Perhaps her greatest achievement though, was that she used the legal process, the very bastion of male privilege, to recover her personal freedom, her wealth and her children, and thus strike a powerful blow in the struggle for equality between men and women in marriage.

Elinor Brent-Dyer and two of her most popular titles.

Elinor M. Brent-Dyer (1894-1969)

Prolific writer, author of the Chalet School Stories

The life of the author of the 'Chalet School' series has been celebrated by three commemorative plaques. These are to be found in the Austrian Tyrol, in Hereford, and on the wall of the school she attended in South Shields, the town where she was born and spent much of her life. Elinor was one of South Shields' most successful and prolific authors.

Elinor Mary Brent-Dyer was born, Gladys Eleanor May Dyer, in 1894. Her home at 52 Winchester Street, South Shields, was a far cry from the opulent houses of her Chalet School pupils. It was a modest terrace house without electricity or hot water and with an outdoor privy. While Elinor's stories tell of large happy families, Elinor herself came from a broken home; her parents separated acrimoniously when she was only three years old, and her mother Nelly was only able to manage financially because her father, a master mariner, had left her a small legacy. Elinor was a bright lively girl and musical, as was her mother, who taught her to play piano. Throughout her life Elinor enjoyed singing and playing the piano and the cello, which she had learned as a teenager. As a toddler she would sit telling stories to the cat for hours.

The small private fee-paying school Elinor attended, St Nicholas' in South Shields, was run in the home of the Misses Alice and Henrietta Stewart, neither of whom had a teaching qualification. Elinor herself said the accent was on good manners rather than academic attainment. Later in her life, Elinor claimed to have attended Dame Allen's school in Newcastle, a prestigious school in the west end of the city, but this was wishful thinking! Elinor had a fairly happy childhood until her dearest school friend, Elizabeth, died of TB in 1911 and a year later her only brother, Henzell, died suddenly of meningitis. Elinor was upset again in June 1913 when her mother remarried. However, Septimus Ainsley, her new stepfather, was a man of substance and the family moved to a much better house, 5, Belgrave Terrace South Shields, with modern facilities and air of middle class respectability. It was a step up the social ladder.

Elinor left the little school in South Shields at eighteen and, after a brief spell of pupil-teaching, went to City of Leeds Teacher Training College in 1915 where, ever creative, she adopted a new name, Patricia Maraquita Dyer! In 1917, when she returned to South Shields as a qualified teacher, she resumed her baptismal names. Elinor taught in local schools but was determined to become a writer, and she changed her name again to a more appropriate, *nom de plume*! It appeared on her one and only passport issued in 1924, and was Elinor Mary Brent-Dyer.

Elinor experimented with many literary forms before she was published. She tried short stories, poetry, and even wrote plays, one of which, *My Lady Caprice*, was successfully staged at the local theatre in 1921. However, her first publication in 1922, *Gerry Goes to School*, was a girls' school story. In the 1920s the girls' schools genre was hugely popular and kept an army of writers feverishly busy, authors like Angela Brazil, Elsie J. Oxenham and Enid Blyton. At the age of twenty-eight, Elinor M. Brent-Dyer was delighted to join them. While *Gerry Goes to School*, the first of three books in the 'La Rochelle' series, sold very well, however, the real turning point of her writing career came a little later when she visited the Austrian Tyrol, Pertisau am Achensee, in 1924.

Overwhelmed by the beauty of the place, she had a brainwave and decided to base a series of Chalet School stories right there on the shores of Lake Tiernsee (real name Achensee) in the stunning mountains of the North Tirol. Her fictional school was established with just three pupils, (Joey, Grizel and Simone) who were then joined by six Tirolean girls, and so the Chalet School series began.

From the outset the Chalet school books were different from other children's series. The beautiful setting, the mixture of nationalities and religions, the family-like atmosphere and the use of foreign phrases, all made for a brilliant read. The air of authenticity was enriched by the relocation of the Chalet school to match international events. The Chalet School in Exile sees the school leaving Austria after the Nazi annexation and relocating to Guernsey. When that became unsafe it was relocated to Armishire (Herefordshire) and finally in *Changes for the Chalet School*, the school settles in Switzerland. Between 1925 and 1970, fifty-eight Chalet School stories were published. They are still in publication today supported by readers from all over the world. The brilliance of the Chalet School series is that over the years Elinor managed to write entertaining stories, full of comedy, fun and adventure as well as maintaining excellent characterisation throughout. Young girls read them in their thousands, partly because they felt they could grow up with the characters, and encouraged by their mothers who delighted in the highly moral tone of the books relieved by a fair scattering of mischief.

In 1925, Elinor moved south to gain more teaching experience and more material for her books. She held teaching posts at St Helen's, Northwood Middlesex, at Moreton House School, Dunstable, Bedfordshire, and in Fareham near Portsmouth. Always a keen musician and a practising Christian, she became a member of the Festival Choir at Fareham. By 1930 she had returned to the family home in South Shields where, at St. Bede's Catholic Church, she was received into the Roman Catholic Faith. This decision may have been influenced by the Catholic liturgies she had enjoyed in Austria.

In 1933 the family moved to Hereford, where she secured a job as a governess. Her stepfather died in 1937 and shortly afterwards Elinor opened a school of her own, The Margaret Roper School. This was not a success. Apart from an inability to attract enough pupils, arrangements within the school left much to be desired. Elinor's mother Nellie, who was everywhere accompanied by at least five cats, was responsible for the school lunches, which it seems were vile! This was a far cry from the pristine arrangements at the Chalet School. By 1948, Elinor could barely keep up with the demand for her books so she closed the school and from then on devoted all her time to writing and writing and more writing. In all Elinor produced over one hundred books.

Nellie, Elinor's mother, died in 1957, and Elinor moved to Redhill, Surrey in 1964 where she lived until her death in 1969. She is buried in Redstone Cemetery (grave number 8326). In her centenary year (1994) the members of the thriving Friends of the Chalet School erected a headstone which they maintain to this day. This group has a world-wide membership, produces a magazine and meets regularly. It owns the copyright of all one hundred of Elinor's books and ensures that the Chalet School series is always in print.

From the outset Gladys Eleanor May Dyer was determined to make her mark in the literary world. Despite the odds being against her, born as she was into poverty and without either connections or money, she used all her energy and creative skills to produce high-quality unique series in the Girls' Schools genre. At least three generations of women have been inspired by her work. Val McDermid, the crime writer, is a great fan and recently Dame Patricia Routledge paid tribute to the Chalet School books, saying that she had never intended to become an actress, she really wanted to be headmistress of the Chalet School! The Chalet School books have become classics in the field of children's literature and Elinor M. Brent-Dyer's legacy is the treasure trove of optimistic and timeless stories she created for her world-wide readership.

Above) Suffragettes at Newcastle
Central Station meet Kathleen
Brown (seated) as she returns to
the city upon her release from
prison in London.
Right) Kathleen Brown.

Kathleen Brown (1887-1973)

Suffragette and Newcastle's first hunger-striker

In Newcastle's handsomest street, Grey Street, there is a plaque on the building - Number 71 - which was once 'The Turk's Head' hotel and where, in 1909, Newcastle suffragettes held a celebratory tea to welcome back local heroine Kathleen Brown shortly after her release from Holloway prison where she had been one of the first suffragettes to go on hunger strike, and the first hunger-striker to be freed. Kathleen had been met with loud cheers at the Central Station by a huge crowd of enthusiastic supporters wearing the purple and green suffragette colours and, apparently, by 3 landaus and 2 brakes!

Indeed Newcastle, along with London, Birmingham and Manchester, has justly been described as one of the principal suffragette cities in the country with some of the movement's most notable activists (such as Emily Wilding Davison and Charlotte Marsh) hailing from the North East as well as Dr Ethel Williams and, later on, Connie Lewcock.

Kathleen Brown was born in 1887 and was the daughter of Joseph and Margaret Brown of Greenside, near Ryton, now part of the Borough of Gateshead. Joseph was a senior North East railway employee, described as an Accountant on Kathleen's wedding certificate. Her mother Margaret by all accounts was a strong character and - in the words of her granddaughter, Ann Moore - had 'an unquestioning assumption of women's equality'. No doubt these views influenced Kathleen and her sisters as they grew up.

Kathleen suffered problems with deafness from her teenage years onwards. This has been attributed to various causes including measles but a letter from

Kathleen's husband Donald written in 1965 describes how Kathleen, as a thirteen year old pupil at Dame Allen's school in Newcastle had her ears regularly boxed 'over a number of months' for failing to do the homework set for the seventeen years olds alongside whom she was placed. This together with a fall from a swing and a slowness to recognise her problem and get it treated worsened the condition considerably. This meant that when she enrolled at Armstrong College, Newcastle (now Newcastle University) to study art she had difficulty in following the lectures. She left and, unusually for a woman at the time, subsequently qualified as a Sanitary Inspector. According to Donald this work led her to be deeply concerned with poor living and working conditions and with child welfare in slum districts. It also marked the time when she became increasingly interested in suffrage issues.

While the date of Kathleen joining the suffragette movement is unclear her increasing involvement dates from 1907-09. 1909 was a particularly momentous year for her. Released from Holloway in July she was, not long after, in October, imprisoned in Newcastle for breaking a window in Pink Lane Post Office at the time of Lloyd George's visit to the city. Visiting Government Ministers were a frequent target of the suffragettes and Lloyd George - then Chancellor of the Exchequer - was the object of their particular ire as it was felt that after initially seeming to support them he had then rejected their cause. His 1909 visit was the focus of national attention and prominent suffragettes Christabel Pankhurst and Lady Constance Lytton had travelled up from London incognito to lend their support to their Newcastle friends. Such was the authorities' concern about suffragette protests that the meeting Lloyd George was to address at the Palace Theatre in the Haymarket was advertised with the warning that no tickets would be sold to women!

Eleven suffragettes including Kathleen and Lady Lytton were arrested and imprisoned as a result of the demonstrations against Lloyd George and together they all wrote a letter to the *Times* saying that in prison they would continue their protest, hold hunger strikes if necessary and giving the government four alternatives: 'to release in a few days; to inflict violence upon our bodies; to add death to the champions of our cause by leaving us to starve; or, and this is the best and only wise alternative, to give women the vote.' The imprisoned women, while subjected to harsh conditions, were aware that demonstrations supporting them were taking place outside. This even included the Jarrow Town Band playing underneath Kathleen's window to cheer her up!

Following a hunger strike Kathleen was released on 21st October. However her year of protest was not over. In December 1909 she was found hiding, with a male supporter of the Women's Social and Political Union (WSPU) in the Queen's Hall in London, once again on the occasion of a planned visit by Lloyd George. Apparently they had managed to pass themselves off as theatre performers to gain access to the building and were only discovered after a day in hiding.

Kathleen's commitment and dedication was recognised with the presentation to her of the suffragette hunger-strike 'For Valour' medal. The citation reads: 'Presented to Kathleen Brown, by the Women's Social and Political Union, in recognition of a gallant action whereby through endurance to the last extremity of hunger and hardship a great principle of political justice was vindicated.'

In total Kathleen was imprisoned three times and took part in numerous, high-profile, suffragette events including with her fellow campaigners commandeering a London Fire Engine and, with Kathleen at the reins, driving it down Tottenham Court Road, fire-bell clanging furiously! There is no doubt that Kathleen's suffragette involvement was very much supported by her mother and indeed by her younger sister Sydney who was frustrated that she was deemed too young to participate fully in the movement. At one demonstration Kathleen's mother Margaret was told by a policeman, 'now Granny, you shouldn't be here, you go off home out of harm's way'. Margaret promptly marched off, picked up a stone and threw it through a window of the Home Office!

Reading about Kathleen's exploits what also comes across strongly are the bonds of comradeship and solidarity which bound the active, campaigning suffragettes, like her, together. They supported each other, particularly when subjected to inhumane treatment in prison. They also celebrated each other's successes and encouraged each other to further action and protest, in pursuit of their cause. Kathleen frequently accompanied Mrs. Pankhurst and her closest supporters on their travels. Mrs. Pankhurst thought highly of her and also claimed that Kathleen made the best cup of tea of all her travelling companions!

Kathleen continued to be active in the suffragette movement up until 1914, particularly in the Doncaster area. She shared a house there - described as a 'veritable suffragette hive' with fellow campaigners Lilian Lenton and Violet Key-Jones. Their role seems to have been one of co-ordinating suffragette activity across Yorkshire. The Doncaster suffragettes were at times victims of the infamous Cat and Mouse Act which released hunger-strikers so that they could recover their strength only to re-imprison them. It was the outbreak of the First World War in 1914 which led to Kathleen ceasing her campaigning, as part of the general suspension of suffragette activities at that time.

Kathleen's great-nephew is Charles Moore, author, official biographer of Margaret Thatcher and former editor of the *Spectator*. He has written of his pride in his great-aunt and described her, charmingly, as 'tiny and brave - with hair so long she could sit on it'. Charles' mother, Ann, remembers first seeing Kathleen when she was a small child and recalling her warm smile and welcoming wave, and her striking auburn hair coiled in a plait around her head.

Kathleen's husband to be, Donald Fraser, recounts meeting Kathleen at a Fabian School in North Wales - a school which had been set up by Kathleen's cousin, Mabel, and George Bernard Shaw. Kathleen and Donald (who was an Indian Civil Service official) married in 1919 at the beautiful medieval church of Bywell St. Peter in the Tyne Valley near Stocksfield where Kathleen's family then lived. After their marriage they were to travel to India together although Kathleen was worried that her prison record could create complications in obtaining a passport, a problem which must have been surmounted as they settled in India afterwards for a number of years, during which time Donald was a District Commissioner. Together too, in 1921, they opened a school there. On leaving India, they moved to Africa and farmed in what was then Rhodesia, followed by a period of residence in Kenya. They finally returned to retire in the UK, in the 1930s, first to Buckinghamshire and later to Ashburton in Devon.

In a long and successful marriage Kathleen and Donald had four children. Donald's pride in his 'darling Kathleen' and her suffragette past is obvious from a letter he wrote at the time of their 46th wedding anniversary in 1965. Although little has been published about Kathleen's later life, not surprisingly her descendants - including son Darien, his wife Jean, and eight grandchildren- are proud of her and maintain a keen interest in her and her suffragette achievements. There is no doubt, too, that her strong commitment to the suffragette cause, and the range of activities she undertook, means that she is still very much remembered not only in her native North East but, rightly, also as part of the history of the wider national suffragette movement across the UK.

A plaque in Grey Street, Newcastle unveiled in March 2017.

Josephine Butler (1828-1906)

Pre-eminent Victorian Social Reformer

'The most distinguished Englishwoman of the 19th Century'

(Millicent Garrett Fawcett)

Josephine Butler's remarkable life began in Milfield, Northumberland, where she was born on 13th April 1828. She was christened Josephine Elizabeth Grey and her father, John Grey, was the cousin of Earl Grey, who as Prime Minister from 1831 to 1834, oversaw the passing of the Great Reform Bill. Like Earl Grey, Josephine's parents were committed to social justice and backed the great reform causes of the day including the abolition of slavery. Unusually for a man of his time John Grey supported the education and political emancipation of women. Such a background meant that Josephine was encouraged to learn about society and government from an early age.

Despite this, and in the light of her comfortable and happy childhood, it would have been

Josephine Butler in her campaigning pose.
(Josephine Butler Society)

likely that Josephine, like other women of her privileged background, would have simply married well and settled into affluent country life. It is astonishing, therefore, how far she departed from that traditional role.

It seems probable that Josephine met her future husband, George Butler, in Durham at the university, where he had been appointed as a classics lecturer after a distinguished academic career at Exeter College, Oxford. They married in St Andrew's Church, Corbridge in 1852, after a year's engagement. An 1851 portrait of Josephine shows a strikingly beautiful woman in a delightfully thoughtful pose.

George turned out to be the perfect spouse for Josephine, supporting her and working with her at every turn, again somewhat remarkable in an age when women were legally their husband's property and had very few rights. Indeed George, in addition to his own academic and clerical roles, was fully associated with the causes Josephine came to be so involved with.

Their first home was at Oxford, where George had been appointed Public Examiner for Schools, and it was there that their two elder children, George and Stanley were born, to be followed eventually by another son Charles and a daughter, Evangeline Mary. Their life at Oxford was happy although bouts of poor health, which beset Josephine throughout her life, occurred there. Significantly one incident aroused Josephine's social conscience and gave an early indication of some of the causes she would subsequently take up. This was the case of a young girl who had been seduced by an Oxford don, had borne his child and as a result had become an outcast. The accepted attitude of the time of blaming and punishing the victim for the crime appalled and outraged Josephine.

Life in Cheltenham, their next home, where George was appointed Deputy Principal at Cheltenham College, began well but was subsequently marred by tragedy when their youngest child - and precious daughter - Eva fell accidentally to her death from the banister near the top of a flight of stairs in their home. Josephine was haunted evermore by the loss of her daughter - 'the brightest of our little circle'. While her religious faith survived this loss, the event seems to have strengthened her resolve to tackle social injustices and suffering, and improve the quality of life for the oppressed.

A new challenge for George opened up in 1866, when he was appointed to be Head of Liverpool College. There Josephine's social involvement began in earnest. She began visiting 'fallen women' - a definition which not only included prostitutes but also unmarried mothers and young girls such as she had encountered in Oxford - and she and George established a 'House of Rest' where they could be offered shelter and a chance to escape poverty and subjection.

At Liverpool she also supported campaigns to admit women to higher education and, together with Anne Clough, she founded the North of England Council for Promoting the Higher Education of Women. Josephine was the Council's first elected President and she held this position from 1867 to 1871. Again in conjunction with Anne Clough, she was involved in setting up the second Women's College in Cambridge, Newnham. Her concern for women's wellbeing also led her to support and campaign for the Married Women's Property Act of 1870 that allowed married women to be the legal owners of the money they earned and to inherit property.

However it was the passing of the Contagious Diseases Acts in 1864, 1866, and 1869 that completely transformed Josephine's life and marked the beginning of her 'Great Crusade'. The Acts, by today's standards and attitudes, are scarcely comprehensible but, given Victorian ideas, for a respectable married woman such as Josephine Butler to speak about them openly in public meetings and campaign against them with such fervour astounded and shocked the society of the time. The social context of the Acts was the concern that soldiers in garrison towns frequently contracted venereal diseases through contact with prostitutes. The 'philosophy' behind the Acts was that soldiers had a right to be served by 'clean' women and the soldiers themselves were exonerated from any responsibility for preventing the spread of disease. The Acts stipulated that prostitutes or those suspected of being prostitutes had to register and be subjected to regular - even fortnightly - internal examinations so that they could be certified disease-free. If it turned out that they were infected they were imprisoned. Women would also be imprisoned if they refused to allow themselves to be examined. These laws were administered by plain clothes policemen and the stories of them harassing women, some of whom were not prostitutes, and harrowing accounts of the actual examinations were legion. There was also no understanding given whatsoever to the circumstances that drove many poor women to prostitution.

Josephine campaigned relentlessly against the Acts and spoke at meetings up and down the country. She spoke to a variety of audiences, but was particularly keen to address meetings of working-class men - and to enlist their sympathy and support - as she knew that it was poverty-stricken women from working class backgrounds who were most at risk of being driven into prostitution and of being treated in this degrading way. She frequently encountered great hostility, and even violence, but she also engendered much warmth, recording that at a meeting in Morpeth 'An allusion I made to my father, speaking of myself as a Northumbrian, was most affectionately responded to. I felt supremely comfortable, for it was a thoroughly Northumbrian atmosphere.'

The campaign to repeal the Acts became highly organised, with Josephine's own flair for organisation being given full rein. Elections and by-elections became occasions for the campaign to support candidates who favoured repeal and oppose those who did not. In 1870, for example, a staunch supporter of the Acts was defeated in Colchester in a by-election - a key moment for Josephine and her supporters.

Josephine's campaigning was not limited to Britain. Indeed the impetus for introducing the Contagious Diseases Acts had been the existence of a similar regime in various parts of Continental Europe and from 1874 onwards Josephine was involved in organising against such measures in France, Switzerland and Italy. After 1879 she increasingly turned her attention to combatting the White Slave Trade whereby women from one country could be kidnapped and forced into prostitution in another. She also campaigned against child prostitution both at home and abroad.

The Contagious Diseases Acts were finally repealed in 1886 but even then Josephine did not rest, despite the fact that she was in poor health and her husband was severely ill. Although the Contagious Diseases Acts had been repealed at home they continued in British India - a situation which Josephine described as 'trampling on the womanhood of a subject race by their conquerors'. Her determination that Indian women should enjoy equal rights to their British counterparts was eventually rewarded by the repeal of the Acts in India in 1895.

In 1896 Josephine Butler published her *Personal Reminiscences of a Great Crusade*, recounting the long campaign to repeal the Contagious Diseases Acts. It is an exciting, unputdownable read that seems, in its description of campaign meetings and Parliamentary manoeuvring, as fresh today as it was then. There is no doubt that Josephine, from all the accounts of her, had remarkable qualities as a public speaker. She spoke quietly, but compellingly. She was not afraid to use humour effectively.

At a meeting of working-class men in the Albert Hall in Sheffield, for example, she described how the Acts represented an attack on poor women by the rich and wealthy. 'If prostitution is a necessity, I call on Mr Cave, Colonel Alexander, and Mr Gathorne Hardy (strong Parliamentary supporters of the Acts) each to contribute a daughter!' Not surprisingly it is reported that the audience erupted into prolonged laughter and cheering!

Josephine had tremendous empathy with women of all backgrounds and circumstances. She deplored the way unmarried middle-class women were belittled because of their single status in a country where the female population outnumbered the male. She opposed the undervaluing of governesses and their relegation to a servant-like status. She raged against the lack of educational and employment opportunities for women in general in the Victorian age. She also was class-blind - at home in all social settings. She was not in the least dazzled by celebrity. Not surprisingly she was an early supporter of women's suffrage and even deplored the French Revolution's 1789 'Rights of Man' Declaration because it did not refer to women too!

Her family life was always important to her and her partnership with George remained rich and close throughout their married life. George's death in 1890 in Winchester - where late in his career he had been made a Canon - deeply affected her but she remained true to the causes they had both held dear saying: 'We who are old cannot run about as we did but at any rate we can think and advise.' Her tenacity and persistence continued to the end.

Josephine died in 1906 and is buried in the tranquil and beautiful churchyard of Kirknewton in the Cheviot Hills. Her grave can be visited there, as can other places in Northumberland associated with her such as St Andrew's Church in Corbridge, where she and George were married and where her parents are buried. It is fitting too, given her commitment to the education of women, that the newest college of Durham University, opened in 2006, is named after her - Josephine Butler College.

A portrait of Josephine Butler by G.F. Watts (RA).

Ivy Close by
Arthur Hacker -
Ferens Art
Gallery.

Ivy Lillian Close (1890-1968)

Britain's First National Beauty Queen and Movie Star

*Born in Portrack to become in 1908 'Most Beautiful woman in the World,'
and outstanding Star in British, American, French and German silent films.*

So reads the plaque mounted on the wall of the Swallow Hotel in Stockton by the British Film Institute, as a commemoration of the centenary of Cinema in 1996.

Britain's first National Beauty Queen, Ivy Close, was born into an ordinary Teesside family in Durham Street, Stockton, one of three children of John Close a jeweller and amateur photographer and his wife Emma, nee Blackburn. From the outset she was extremely pretty with curly blonde hair, a porcelain complexion, sparkling eyes and a sweet smile. When she was eighteen, in 1908, her father sent her photograph to the Daily Mirror's 'Most Beautiful Woman in the World Competition', the first competition of its kind. There were over 1,500 contestants and Ivy scooped first prize. She won a Rover motor car and had her portrait painted by Sir Arthur Hacker. It was exhibited at the Royal Academy in London. In the year of her triumph, the picture filled the entire front page of the *Daily Mirror*, with other pictures of her inside the paper in '*a variety of charming poses*'. The paper was a sell out and Ivy Close became a star overnight. Very soon her image seemed to be everywhere, on birthday cards, postcards, and romanticised photographs and posters. They are now collectors' items.

In 1910, Ivy married the society photographer, Elwin Neame, who had photographed the finalists in the beauty competition and once more our beautiful heroine was front page news. The marriage was a happy one and the couple had two sons.

Elwin supported Ivy in her ambition to break into the silent movie industry, still in its infancy, and her break came when the legendary producer Cecil Hepworth gave her a twelve-month contract. She then set up her own production company, Close films in 1914, one of the first movie production companies founded by a film star. It pre-dated by five years United Artists, the independent Hollywood Company formed by Chaplin, Pickford, Griffith and Fairbanks.

Ivy was not merely a beautiful woman, she was ambitious too, and in 1917, in search of a still broader canvas, she travelled to Jacksonville, Florida, a centre of film making at that time. There she became even more successful as a silent movie actress. In all, Close acted in forty-four films between 1912 and 1929, her most memorable role was in the epic French film, *La Roué* (*The Wheel*), made in 1923. It is still available on DVD today. Jean Paul Cocteau said of it, 'There is cinema before and after *La Roué*, as there is painting before and after Picasso.' Directed by Abel Gance, who also directed the epic film *Napoleon,* it was hailed as an all-round master piece, revolutionary in its day using new lighting techniques and rapid scene changes and cuts.

Tragically Elwin was killed in a road accident in 1923, leaving Ivy with two boys to bring up at a time when the advent of talking movies was diminishing Close's acting opportunities as fewer silent movies were being made. Her film career ended when her English accent was deemed unsuitable for American audiences, and although Ivy continued to star in pantomime and minor films for a while, by the end of the 1920s she had fallen off the radar.

Ivy's career may have ended in the 1920s but the family dynasty she and Elwin Neame launched is still going strong. Their son Ronald Neame, directed *The Poseidon Adventure*, and *The Prime of Miss Jean Brodie*, their grandson was a Bafta nominated writer and producer and Gareth Neame her great grandson devised the idea for *Downton Abbey*.

In 1938, Ivy married Curly Baston, the Australian-born make-up artist and stuntman who died in 1957. Ivy died in a nursing home in Oxfordshire in 1968. She left over forty silent movies. In 1996 her son unveiled a plaque commemorating her very considerable contribution to the development of the international film industry.

Somehow Sir Arthur Hacker's Portrait of Ivy Close was lost for several years and has only recently been discovered in the collection of the Ferens Art Gallery in Hull. It has now been restored and is on display again, a return to the limelight for the girl from the North East who optimised her chances and became one of Britain's first modern celebrities.

Grace Colman
(1892-1971)

MP, Educator and
Defender of Animal Rights

Grace Colman, MP for Tynemouth 1945.

Grace Colman was not born or brought up in the North East and only served as Member of Parliament for Tynemouth for five years. She was, however, very much an adopted daughter of the region who loved Tyneside and Northumberland and for whom the North East became home. Although utterly devoted to - and tireless in her efforts on behalf of her constituency, she also made an important contribution to wider national causes she felt passionately about, including both women's education and the cause of animal welfare, of which she was an early and effective champion.

Grace was born in 1892 into a clerical family, the daughter of a Canon of Worcester Cathedral, Frederick Selincourt Colman. She was educated at home by governesses along with her brothers and sisters. That home education must have been of a good standard since in 1914 she won a scholarship to Newnham College Cambridge, where she took Honours in History and Economics in the Tripos, parts I and II. She also distinguished herself in sport, being a member of the first Women's Eight to row on the Cam and becoming President of the Women's Rowing Club.

Although brought up in a Conservative family, during her time in Cambridge Grace's political outlook changed and by 1916 she had joined the Labour Party. In her studies she had concentrated on social and industrial policy, on the problems of unemployment and on the possibilities offered by different forms of co-operative production. These interests became the subjects she specialised in on becoming Tutor in history and economics at Ruskin College, Oxford, (from 1920-1925) and on being appointed staff Tutor for tutorial classes in the University of London (1925-1940). Her London post, where she was responsible for classes arranged jointly with the Workers' Educational Association, also led to her being asked to lecture elsewhere in the UK, including the Midlands and the North East.

During this time, Grace undertook many tasks on behalf of the Labour Party including lecturing at the summer schools organised for women members. She relished this work, as she found it deeply satisfying to engage with women who were both keen to learn and who had had little formal education. Her ability to explain complex issues in straightforward and clear language was legendary and at every stage she encouraged her students to ask questions and engage in discussions on the issues raised. Her national reputation within the Labour Movement and her work for the summer schools were recognised when she was asked (in 1940) to Chair the 20th National Conference of Labour Women.

During the 1930s, Grace also spoke on international issues and was an early opponent of the policy of appeasement. She urged the building up of a peace front of countries opposed to Nazism and called for a policy of 'making it clear to Hitler that aggression will be effectively resisted'. During the war she was an ARP warden in west London and worked as a temporary civil servant with the Ministry of Labour and the Board of Trade.

Grace had been adopted as prospective Labour Candidate for Tynemouth in 1939 but because of the Second World War general elections were postponed until 1945, when, as part of the large-scale Labour victory, she was elected with a majority of over 3000. Grace campaigned ceaselessly but without fuss. She particularly disliked trivial publicity. In one of her earlier campaigns she had - perhaps not surprisingly - rejected a campaign slogan suggested by her election agent 'Vote for Colman, she's Mustard'. Neither did she like the suggestion by a youthful Tynemouth supporter of the line 'Vote for Colman, she's hot stuff!'

She did not want to exploit the fact, intriguing to some, that she was the cousin of the Hollywood star - and heart-throb - Ronald Colman.

Once elected, she declared in her victory speech 'Constant complaints have reached me that people were not able to get problems dealt with. That won't happen again. I pledge myself to be worthy of your confidence and face up to the responsibilities.' All the testimonies to her as a model constituency representative demonstrated that she lived up to her pledge. Unlike her predecessor, who apparently in twenty-one years of representing the constituency had hardly ever spoken in Parliament, she lost no time in making her maiden speech at Westminster in which she spoke passionately about the hardships and dangers faced by North Shields fishermen. She also raised her concerns about the fishing industry in debates on the 1948 White Fish and Herring Industries Bill and in the 1949 Sea Fish Industry Bill.

Grace can be considered one of the pioneers of animal welfare. She was one of the chief supporters of the Protection of Animals (Hunting and Coursing Prohibition) Bill of 1948, describing hare coursing as 'a most brutal sport' and declaring that 'in a civilised society it must be recognised that animals do not exist merely for our own profit and pleasure'. She was also concerned about the welfare of pet animals and in the Pet Animals bill spoke up for controls on how and where such animals could be sold - arguing that it must be from licensed premises or from outlets that had to respect high standards of accommodation for the animals concerned.

Grace turned down the offer of a Parliamentary Commission to India from Prime Minister Attlee, which would have meant a promotion for her and a recognition of her abilities, in order to concentrate on local and constituency matters. Perhaps if her Parliamentary career had been longer the pressure on her to accept a Ministerial appointment might have become irresistible, but there can be little doubt that her commitment to representing the people who had elected her would have remained her principal motivation and would have been sufficient reward in itself. John Sleight in his book 'Women on the March' aptly describes her as 'one of the outstanding women politicians never to become a Government Minister, though it was largely her own choosing.'

Grace lived at 5 Kitchener Terrace, North Shields, always in the company of a well-loved pet dog. She is remembered as being endearingly unfashionable turning up, for example, at summer garden parties and 'stumping about' in a tweed skirt and brogues amidst the summer frocks and lightweight suits that everyone else was wearing. She was a private person yet was also very loyal to her friends and received loyalty in return.

Grace Colman lost her Tynemouth seat in 1950 and again, when she tried to re-take it, in 1951. This was not just because of the national swing but also followed boundary changes that had added substantial Conservative-voting coastal areas to her constituency. She was defeated by the Conservative politician, Irene Ward.

For a while, Grace returned to London and worked for the Labour Party as an editor of educational publications. She returned to live permanently in the North East in 1961, lecturing for the Workers' Educational Association and undertaking work for the Royal Society for the Prevention of Cruelty to Animals. She also became involved in the United Nations Association and a number of other organisations linked to the causes she held dear.

From reminiscences of those who knew her, Grace was kind and compassionate, but without sentimentality. She sought to change the conditions that led to social disadvantage. She was blazingly honest, forthright - sometimes disconcertingly so - and intellectually rigorous. In conversation she challenged your ideas and lifted your sights. Gordon Adam, former MEP for Northumbria and former Mayor of North Tyneside, described her as being both extraordinarily open-minded and able as well as being extremely thorough in her investigation of every topic.

Grace died in 1971 aged seventy-nine and left legacies to Animal Charities, the NSPCC, the Save the Children Fund and the regional Labour Party. Her ashes were scattered in the Northumbrian uplands in a place where she had loved to walk with her dogs.

Grace touched many people's lives through her educational and political work. Although there is no plaque commemorating her at present, a Grace Colman award was established by the Northumberland Labour Women's Advisory Council, providing an annual scholarship to attend the women's summer schools, where Grace had shown herself to be such an outstanding and inspirational lecturer over many years.

Ida Cook (1904-1986) &
Louise Cook (1901-1991)

Opera Buffs and Heroines of the Holocaust

This is the remarkable story of two apparently ordinary sisters. Born in Sunderland, they lived in Alnwick from 1912 until 1919, and both girls spent their formative years at the Duchess school in Alnwick. Although their father was posted to Wandsworth in 1919, the family never lost touch with their friends in the North. On leaving school, both girls followed in their father's footsteps and joined the civil service, Louise as a clerical assistant at the Board of Education and Ida as a copy typist. Both girls earned less than £3 a week.

Who could have predicted from these unexceptional beginnings, that these 'ordinary girls' would travel all over America and Europe to hear opera and become close friends with many international opera stars, and that through this love of opera they would rescue twenty-nine Jewish people from the horrors of Nazi Germany and facilitate the release of dozens more. Who would have guessed that Ida would become a successful and prolific writer, financing their rescue missions by writing romantic novels under the pseudonym Mary Burchell and that in later life Ida, this 'ordinary girl,' a co- founder of the Romantic Novelists Association, would become its President from 1965 until her death in 1986.

In her autobiography. Ida describes the family of two girls and two boys as a close knit, loving and Christian family, whose parents instilled in them a clear sense of right and wrong, which served them in good stead throughout life. The sisters had complimentary personalities. Louise was quiet, thoughtful and the more intellectual of the two, it was she who taught herself German the better to deal with the refugees and German authorities. Ida, on the other hand, was practical, very sociable and loquacious, a great organiser. Both sisters were resourceful, cheerful, optimists.

Their love of opera started when Louise bought a gramophone on hire purchase in 1923. Their collection of classical discs included Amelita Galli-Curci singing *Un Bel Di Vedremo*, from *Madame Butterfly*. Both girls were absolutely smitten by the aria and, in particular, by the voice of Galli-Cucci. The next step was to go to Covent Garden to hear live opera and they loved it. They queued every night of the season to get into the cheapest seats in the gallery and soon became regulars, standing at the stage door trying to get the autographs of the lead singers. Ida even bought a box brownie to take photographs of their operatic idols.

Their infatuation with the voice of Amelita Galli-Curci led them to form a plan to travel to New York to hear her live even though they had no money. They wrote to tell Galli-Curci of their plans, and she replied to them. Over the next two years, each girl saved hard and so it was that the Cook sisters who had never even been to Brighton unaccompanied, travelled third class to New York on the *Berengaria* in December 1926 to hear Galli-Curci sing at the Metropolitan Opera House

They had a whale of a time. Amelita Galli-Curci entertained them and gave them access to all her performances as she had promised. The success of their trip to New York and their new-found friendship with Galli-Curci inspired both girls to do more travelling but they were still each only earning £3 per week. Resourceful as ever, Ida decided to try writing. She sent off a breezy little article to *Mabs Fashions*, describing her use of their patterns to make their clothes for the New York trip. *Mabs Fashions* printed the article and encouraged Ida to write more for them. From 1925 until 1934, Ida wrote enough articles and short stories to enable her to resign from the civil service and for the pair of them to go to America, Verona, Amsterdam, Vienna and Florence to hear opera. During this period, they became fans of and then close friends with the American soprano Rosa Ponselle.

1934 was a turning point for the sisters. It was the year Ida began to write romantic novels for Mills and Boon and soon she was earning £1000 a year. That same year they made their first visit to the Salzburg Music Festival and met Frau Mitia Meyer, a Jewish musicologist, who explained to them plight of Jews under Hitler. In 1935, when the Nazis enacted the Nuremburg Laws depriving all German Jews of their rights as citizens, the sisters decided they must help. They determined to use the Guarantee Visa system to save as many Jews as they could. Under this system, the Nazi authorities allowed the

Ida and Louise Cook about to board at TWA flight.

departure of Jews to Britain if they had a guarantee of financial support there. Ida set about writing as many as three or four books a year, for now she saw the need for money as a matter of life and death, to provide guarantees for escaping Jews.

From 1935 until war broke out the sisters' opera trips were confined to Germany and became a cover for rescue missions. Since they were already known at Cologne airport and in Vienna as the young English women with a passion for opera, their visits were at first seen as unremarkable. When controls became more stringent, the sisters would go in by one frontier and out by another, they would travel one way by air and home by train and boat.

They received the names of desperate Jewish families from Mitia Mayer and from Frau Jack, a contact in Frankfurt, who collated lists of potential families for them to interview in Mayer's home in Frankfurt. In essence, when they received a request, say from a man who had been sentenced to go to Buchenwald Concentration camp in a few weeks or days and whose only hope was escape to England, they would work night and day to try and sort out his papers and raise money for a guarantee.

To help provide refugees with money they smuggled their money and their transportable wealth out for them. Reselling these valuable items gave the refugees a source of income in England, which made it easier to get the guarantors required. Ida also gave talks all around the country, encouraging people to act as guarantors and they bought a flat to act as a haven for refugees newly arrived in England.

Although protected by their British passports the sisters were often in real danger. On their last visit to Berlin before war broke out, having already rescued his parents they rescued Walter Stiefel, a member of the Anti-Hitler underground for six years. If he had been caught and made to talk the sisters would certainly have been arrested.

In all, Ida and Louise Cook raised twenty-nine financial guarantees and arranged the safe passage of 29 German and Austrian Jews. One of their final cases was the rescue of Frau Mitia's daughter, Elsa Mayer Lismann. Elsa was the last of her family to escape.

Their rescue work stopped when war was declared and they could no longer travel. During the war Louise's office was evacuated to Wales, while Ida was assigned superintendent of a night shelter in Bermondsey, South London. After the war the sisters resumed life with their customary vigour and enthusiasm. Their refugee work continued with the 'Adoption Committee for Aid to Displaced Persons,' which involved mostly fund-raising.

Ida continued to write throughout the rest of her life. In all she wrote over 100 romantic novels for Mills and Boon between 1935 and 1985. In 1965 she began work on her famous Warrander Saga, a series of thirteen books about the world of the opera and concert hall. The last was published in 1985. Ida's literary masterpiece was, however, her autobiography. First published in 1950, as *We Followed Our Stars*, it was reissued in 1980 as *Safe Passage*. It is still in print and widely read.

The sisters remained passionate about opera and continued their travels until old age defeated them. At the age of eighty-two, Ida died from cancer and in 1991 Louise died from septicaemia. Unfortunately, all the papers from before the war, all the letters and photographs from the many families asking for help were destroyed by Louise when Ida died. No one knows why.

In 1965 the Yad Vashem Holocaust Memorial Authority in Jerusalem honoured these brave, energetic and enthusiastic sisters, about whose lives there was nothing 'ordinary', with the title, *Righteous among the Nations* and in 2010 the sisters were each honoured posthumously as, 'A British Hero of the Holocaust,' by the British Government. In January 2017, on Holocaust Memorial Day, Sunderland Town Council unveiled a blue plaque in memory of Ida and Louise Cook, at their birthplace, Croft Avenue, Chester Road, Sunderland. It reads,

'Ida Cook (1904-1986) and her sister Louise Cook (1901-1991), residents of 37 Croft Avenue, Sunderland, saved many Jews from persecution. In 1965 they were honoured as Righteous among Nations by the state of Israel. Under the pen name Mary Burchell, Ida was a prolific author for Mills and Boon.'

Here is proof of what 'ordinary' girls can achieve.

Catherine Cookson (1906-1998)

Best-selling Author

At the height of her fame, Catherine Cookson was Britain's best-selling author and one of Britain's richest women. Her books have been regularly amongst the top ten most popular library books borrowed and for nineteen years, from 1984 to 2003, she was number one on that list. Given her impoverished and difficult childhood, her lack of formal education and the health problems - both physical and psychological - that she had had to battle with, her achievements are astonishing. Often caricatured as lightweight women's romances, her works are rooted in the history and day-to-day reality of her native Tyneside and show a deep knowledge of its industrial, economic and social evolution.

Catherine was born in Tyne Dock and brought up there and in East Jarrow. She was the illegitimate daughter of Kate Fawcett, the woman who, until Catherine was seven years old, she thought was her older sister. Catherine lived with Kate and Kate's parents, her grandmother and step-grandfather Rose and John McMullen. During her childhood Catherine was known as Katie McMullen. The family were in almost continuous financial difficulties, well paid permanent jobs being difficult to come by, and these problems were exacerbated by both her mother and her grandfather's partiality to alcohol. There were also tensions between Kate and her parents, her parents not wanting Kate to have any motherly responsibilities for her daughter and wanting to deny Catherine's real parentage at every opportunity. Not surprisingly the relationship between Catherine and Kate was fraught.

Catherine's autobiography *Our Kate* is a vivid portrayal of her childhood. At times money was so short that Catherine was a regular, even weekly, visitor, to the local pawnbroker on behalf of the family. At times she scavenged for coal by following a coal man's cart and picking up any coke that was spilled. From age seven or eight she was also regularly sent to the local pub with a flagon to be filled with beer for her mother and step-grandfather, an errand that filled her with shame and dread of the drunkenness and alcoholism that ensued. The paucity of her education is also revealed in her description of poor quality schooling, occasionally relieved by small acts of kindness by individual teachers who recognised perhaps her incipient talent and her fondness for stories and words. Above all, however, the autobiography graphically illustrates how deep the stigma attached to illegitimacy was in those days and how constantly and unfairly, the innocent child of a union outside wedlock was held personally to blame. The casual cruelty frequently inflicted by other children's taunts 'you've got no da' caused deep mental scars that were difficult to overcome, although they perhaps help explain Catherine's determination to create a new life where her family circumstances would not be known or would be irrelevant. In old age Catherine frequently mused on the huge social transformation that had taken place during her lifetime from the social ostracism that illegitimacy involved during her childhood to the widespread acceptance of unmarried couples living together and having children either before marriage or indeed without any marriage ever taking place.

Catherine left school at fourteen and took a series of jobs before beginning a more settled period as a laundry checker at the Harton Workhouse in South Shields. She worked for six years there, saving and scrimping where possible, but decided to move when, despite her work record, she was more than once overlooked for promotion. She opted to try her luck away from Tyneside and moved south, eventually obtaining a post as head of the laundry of the workhouse in Hastings. It was here that her life began to take a very different turn.

As a child Catherine had always been a raconteur. Largely deprived of books, her prized possession was a copy of *Grimm's Fairy Tales* given to her by a neighbour. She liked to write poetry as well as prose and, aged just eleven, she sent a story she had written to the *Shields Gazette* in South Shields. Apparently because of its length, it was rejected for publication. When working at Harton she became a keen user of her local library, which, in many ways, became her substitute for a formal higher education.

She was very conscious of what she felt were her educational shortcomings

A portrait of
Catherine Cookson,
1950.

and apparently, on moving south, took lessons to try to lose her Geordie accent which, it was claimed, was so strong that she had difficulty in making herself understood!

During her first years in Hastings she used savings and the security of insurance policies to buy a large, but very rundown, house with the aim of taking in lodgers or running a home for people with the kind of problems she had encountered in the workhouses. For a while she also tried to reconcile with her mother Kate who, like Catherine, also took in lodgers. One of the lodgers, Tom Cookson, was a grammar school teacher with whom Catherine fell in love and would eventually marry, despite the efforts of her mother and friend to separate them. As an Oxford-educated teacher, Tom was supportive of Catherine's writing and, while not dampening her originality, helped with grammar and use of language.

In Hastings she joined a writers' circle, which also gave her some much needed encouragement.

Catherine married Tom in 1940 at the age of thirty-four. It was a happy and solid partnership that would last almost sixty years. Nonetheless it was a union that had to face many challenges. Tom was involved in war service at the beginning and Catherine had three miscarriages, after which she was told that there should be no more attempts to have children. Physically she had to cope with the effects of what would later be diagnosed as a hereditary blood disorder that had caused problems from her childhood onwards. Mentally the painful legacy of that childhood caught up with her and she succumbed to depression. Treatment for her psychiatric problems included electric shocks and some voluntary stays in hospital. To add to her difficulties she was also undergoing a crisis of faith, turning away from the Catholicism of her youth. She managed to deal with these issues openly and honestly including in her writing which was attracting more attention and through a broadcast for the BBC where she talked about her problems in a way designed to help others experiencing similar difficulties. Catherine occupied her mind with various new activities discovering, in addition to prose and poetry, a talent for drawing. Her first novel. *Kate Hannigan*, was published in 1950. Over the next forty years she was to publish almost 100 books, sell over 100 million copies and be translated into more than twenty languages. While her efforts to educate herself and improve her literary grasp had undoubtedly borne fruit, she drew inspirational strength from her background and experience of life in the North, realising that it was these things that made her writing unique. In her own words 'I had to face the fact that I wouldn't write a word that anyone would really want to read until I threw off the pseudo-lady and accepted my early environment, me grandma, the pawn, the beer carrying, the cinder picking,

Kate's drinking and of course my birth, for it was these things that had gone to make me. Also to own up to being a Northerner and all that this implied'. Over the years many of her novels were dramatised on radio and television. They are well suited to such adaptations as they rely so much on plot and dialogue rather than on nuances or irony or on the introspective musings of characters. Her books continue to sell today and many of the TV adaptations are still widely viewed and broadcast.

Catherine's later years in Hastings were marked by a gradual change in her complex relationship with her alcoholic mother, Kate. Kate stayed with Catherine for the last three years of her life and - particularly with the help of Tom - a closer relationship between mother and daughter emerged. Drinking became less of a problem and Kate obviously relished the fame and success of her daughter. Yet it was only when Catherine was nearly fifty and her mother over seventy with not long to live that Catherine felt able to call her 'Mam' for the first time. Kate died at Catherine and Tom's second house in Hastings, *Loreto*, a house that they had fallen in love with and acquired in 1954. In 1976, Catherine and Tom moved permanently back to the North East, living in Corbridge, then near Hexham and finally - to have easy access to medical treatment - in Jesmond, Newcastle. It was notable that although Catherine's north eastern childhood held many unhappy memories, she had a deep love for the region and its people and treasured its heritage and countryside. Her final years in Northumberland and Newcastle were stable and contented, with, of course, total financial security. Catherine was generous with her money funding research at Newcastle University, supporting local hospitals and giving substantial funds to cultural projects - including the Hatton Gallery - and projects aimed at helping the young people of the region. Many honours came her way. She was made an OBE in 1985 and became Dame Catherine in 1993. She was awarded an honorary degree from Newcastle University and given the Freedom of the borough of South Tyneside. Despite years of ill health, Catherine lived until a few weeks short of her ninety-second birthday. Her beloved husband Tom survived her by just seventeen days. She is remembered in a number of different ways, particularly through her foundation and her bequests, which continue to support good causes particularly in the North East. There is also a Catherine Cookson memorial garden on the site of South Tyneside Hospital, which itself was on the site of the Harton workhouse where Catherine had worked between 1924 and 1929. However it is through her written works above all that her links with the North East and its people live on.

A portrait of
Grace Darling.

RNLI

Grace Darling (1815-1842)

Heroine

Grace Darling was the first and the most feted Victorian heroine, her name became and remains synonymous with outstanding courage and bravery.

Grace Horsley Darling was born in 1815 and lived all her short life on the Farne Islands, a group of twenty-eight wild and beautiful islands lying two miles off the coast from Bamburgh in the North Sea. Many of the islands are submerged at high tide, making the seas around them a notorious hazard for shipping.

Grace was the seventh of the nine children of William Darling, lighthouse keeper, and his wife Thomasina. Until she was ten, the family lived in a small cottage attached to the lighthouse on Brownsman Island. As the only inhabitants of the island, they had to be virtually self-sufficient. Coarse grass offered grazing for a few goats, sheep and rabbits and the soil, enriched by the sea birds, was good enough for the family to grow vegetables. Fish were plentiful, and a pond attracted wildfowl, including the famous Eider or 'cuddy' ducks. Other vital items, such as fresh water, were brought from the mainland.

Although the waters were dangerous, the children were well trained in handling the family coble (a small, flat-bottomed sea-going boat) and in reading the tides and currents. They would explore the rocks and coves, go fishing and collect birds' eggs to eat.

Grace had no formal schooling. Her parents were her teachers. Devoutly

Christian, bible instruction and frequent acts of worship were regular features of their lives. The children were well grounded in the lives of the Northumbrian Saints, Oswald, Aidan and of course Cuthbert, who himself had lived on the Inner Farne. Music played an important part in their lives too. William Darling was a talented folk fiddler and Grace was known to have a lovely singing voice.

The family moved to Longstone Island in 1825 when Brownsman Lighthouse, in the middle of the Farnes, was replaced by Longstone Lighthouse on the eastern extremity of the Farnes. Whilst Longstone Lighthouse provided better accommodation for the family, the island itself was a desolate outcrop of bare rock and to maintain their food source they had to make daily boat trips to Brownsman Island, a mile away.

By the time she was nineteen, the older children had left home and Grace was effectively William's assistant lighthouse keeper. She was devoted to her father and they made an excellent team and although conditions were spartan and secluded, Grace enjoyed her life and had no wish to change it.

In 1838, however, with the sinking of the *Forfarshire* and her heroic courage in the rescue of nine survivors, everything was to change.

Launched in1834, the SS *Forfarshire* was an early luxury paddle boat, built for regular runs between Hull and Dundee and said to be unsinkable! On September 5th 1838, it set off from Hull with cargo and about sixty passengers and crew. On the morning of September 7th the vessel lost power and began to drift uncontrollably towards the Farnes. It was a fierce night with gale force winds, and at 4 am, on Sept 8th the steamship hit Big Harcar rock, about a mile from the Longstone Lighthouse. Within fifteen minutes, the ship broke in two and the back half was swept away with forty-eight people aboard, only nine of whom were later rescued. Meanwhile the forward section of the boat stuck on the rock and was disintegrating rapidly, so the survivors decided to jump and cling onto Big Harcar rock itself, in hope of getting help.

That night only Grace and her parents were in the lighthouse. At 4.45 a.m. Grace saw the wreck and alerted her father. At first they saw no signs of life but then Grace saw survivors clinging to the rocks. William felt the sea was too rough for the life boat at North Sunderland to reach the Harcar rock in time, and so the two of them decided they must at least attempt a rescue in their own twenty-one foot coble, although really it required four oarsmen.

When they set out they knew that, even if they reached the survivors, the two of them alone would never make it back to the lighthouse rowing against the full force of the gale. They gambled on some of the survivors being crewmen fit enough to assist them.

When they reached Harcar Rock, they found nine people alive; a Mrs Dawson, clutching her two dead children, an injured man, seven crewmen and the body of a clergyman. William had to leave the boat to assist the survivors, which left Grace alone to handle the boat and keep it from being smashed on the reef.

As the coble could only take five on board, they decided to take the injured man and the woman, and three of the crew back to the Lighthouse and then repeat the journey. Their gamble had paid off the rescued crewmen were able to assist with the oars while Grace attended to the grieving mother and the injured sailor. On the second journey William took two of the rescued men as crew while Grace remained to assist her mother with the survivors. Miraculously the four remaining men were also saved. It was two more days before the storm abated.

Local and then national newspaper reporters were quickly on the scene, *The Times*, and *The Illustrated London News* among them. And so began a media frenzy. A local reporter wrote that survivors wept as they told of the young woman in a rowing boat who had saved them. *The Times* wrote, 'Is there in the whole field of history, or of fiction, even one instance of female heroism to compare with this?' William's involvement received little comment in the press. The media were captivated by Grace's story, it was all about Grace and she became a media celebrity overnight. News of her outstanding courage spread like wildfire. Newspapers around the world trumpeted her bravery, books, plays and poems praised her selfless courage. As well as some notable portraits, artist after artist painted the violence of the storm, the wreckage of the vessel, the terror of the survivors and the heroism of Grace and her father in the teeth of the tempest.

The involvement of a twenty-two year old girl in such a dangerous rescue was especially sensational because generally Victorian women's lives were constrained by society, they were the weaker vessel, designed to be only wives and mothers! Another ninety years would pass before women were enfranchised! Selfless and brave, Grace herself remained modest. She wrote 'I thank God who enabled me to do so much. I thought it a duty, as no assistance could be had, but still feel sorry I could not do more.'

Almost immediately Grace and her father were awarded £10 each and a silver medal for gallantry by the National Institution for the Preservation of Life from Shipwreck, known today as the RNLI. Grace was the first woman to be honoured in such a way. The Royal Humane Society also awarded Gold Medals to father and daughter. The nineteen year old Queen Victoria, crowned only weeks before, sent Grace a personal letter and a gift of £50. Later the Poet Laureate, William Wordsworth, dedicated a lyrical ballad to her. These accolades and widespread press coverage meant that Grace's fame became international. Newspaper accounts appeared in Europe, America, Japan and

Australia. Well-wishers sent her money and very soon over £1,000 had been donated to Grace. She received hundreds of letters every day, boatloads of visitors arrived at Longstone, hoping to catch a glimpse of her. She was under constant pressure to sit for portraits, to make guest appearances, to open events, to send her autograph and locks of hair or pieces of her clothing.

Naturally shy and retiring, Grace found the intrusion of the public increasingly difficult to deal with, but somehow she coped until in 1842, four years after the heroic rescue, Grace became unwell and developed a persistent cough.

The Duke and Duchess of Northumberland sent their physician to attend her. He diagnosed tuberculosis. Grace was moved to Bamburgh, to the familiar home of her favourite sister Thomasina. There, on the evening of Thursday October 20th 1842, Grace died peacefully in her father's arms at the age of twenty seven.

Grace was buried in St Aidan's churchyard in Bamburgh and two years later an ornate memorial was erected and a fine stained glass window installed in the church to commemorate her.

Grace Darling's bravery has resulted in a considerable legacy. Apart from the many books, paintings and artefacts that she inspired, there is now a Grace Darling Museum in Bamburgh. Perhaps most notably, Grace has become the iconic figurehead of the Royal National Lifeboat Institution, which, since its foundation, has saved over 137,000 lives. Her brave actions continue to inspire the volunteer crews, the men and women who man the lifeboats around the coasts of the British Isles and risk their lives to help others, just as she did 180 years ago.

LONGSTONE LIGHT

BAMBOROUGH

GRACE
DARLING'S
MONUMENT

GRACE
DARLING

Clockwise from top left: 1) A portrait of Grace Darling. 2) Engravings of Grace's life - the Longstone Light, Bamburgh and her monument. 3) The rescue and Grace Darling's image were used on hundreds of commercial items - in this case fittingly- Lifebouy soap.

Girton College

Emily Davies by Rudolph
Lehmann - Girton College,
Cambridge.

Emily Davies (1830-1921)

Pioneer of Women's Higher Education

'The Greatest Feminist of them all'

On the corner of Bensham Road and Rectory Road in Gateshead there is a blue plaque that reads: 'Emily Davies (1830-1921). A pioneer of women's education and the campaign for votes for women. Founder of Girton College, Cambridge. She was a daughter of the Rector of Gateshead and lived her early life in the Rectory that stood on this site.'

Emily Davies' formative years were spent in Gateshead and her experiences, both within her own family and in the town itself, were key influences on her thinking and on her subsequent involvement in public life. She arrived in Gateshead at the age of ten and lived there until settling in London for family reasons in 1860, some twenty years later. Emily was the fourth of a family of five and early on became acutely aware that her three brothers were benefitting from a formal education at school and university whereas she and her sister had to be satisfied with lessons at home, and lessons, moreover, that were deemed appropriate for clergymen's daughters destined for lives of narrow domesticity. Yet Emily from an early age had a keen thirst for knowledge and longed to read widely.

Emily was also an intrepid explorer with a taste for adventure and for finding out about her surroundings. The Rectory was in a populous area of Gateshead and in between meal times - and without her mother suspecting - Emily would roam all over the town including its poorest and meanest neighbourhoods. Emily's biographer, Daphne Bennett, claims that 'before she was twelve she knew every inch of the town, including the slums, very well indeed.' Dismay at the poverty and squalor she encountered engendered in her a keen sympathy for those whose lives were so badly marred and the poverty of women in particular, trying to look after children, while often being obliged to work for a pittance, left an indelible impression on her. She often referred to these youthful experiences in her later campaigning work.

In Gateshead, Emily also made friendships with like-minded girls. Notable among them were Anna Richardson, of a Quaker family (and related by marriage to Anna Richardson the anti-slavery campaigner), and sisters Annie and Jane Crow who lived at Unsworth Hall. Through the Crow sisters Emily also met another key friend, Elizabeth Garrett, later the first woman to study medicine in the UK and become a practising doctor. In later life Emily and Lizzie worked together to promote the cause of women's higher education.

Not long before leaving Gateshead for London, at the age of twenty-eight, Emily's concern for the working conditions of women on Tyneside who were employed in sweated labour led her to find out what more suitable work might be available for them by devising and sending out a questionnaire. Ironically the replies she received were addressed to the Rev. S.E. Davies as the idea that a woman could have taken such an initiative was obviously unthinkable!

The move to London in 1860 was occasioned by the death of Emily's father. Emily's eldest brother, Llewelyn, also a clergyman, was already established in a parish in Marylebone and he and his wife were keen to have Emily and their widowed mother near to them. Llewelyn was to prove not only a loving brother but also a constant support to Emily in her future work. Emily was a fond aunt to Llewelyn and Mary's children.

London allowed Emily to renew her friendship with Lizzie Garrett. Lizzie was facing countless obstacles in her quest to study medicine and Emily was determined both to support her and to open doors to other would-be women students.

Another friend from earlier days, Barbara Bodichon, would also become a key associate of Emily's in this work.

Emily became involved in the National Association for the Promotion of Social Science and presented a paper on 'Medicine as a Profession for Women'. She also worked on *The English Woman's Journal* - a campaigning journal that promoted not only women's education but also their rights to property and their right to vote. As well as firming up her convictions, this period of her life also reveals her growing competence in organisation and her ability to inspire and to lead.

Her first real campaigning project was a crusade to allow girls as well as boys to take the Oxford and Cambridge 'Local Examinations' which were the forerunners of 'O' and 'A' levels. The idea met with considerable opposition but also, thanks to Emily's powers of persuasion and persistence, some strong support. Emily's efforts and those of key allies, including Cambridge graduate Henry Tomkinson and three of Emily's schoolmistress friends, led to the Cambridge Examinations being opened to women on an experimental basis in 1863 and then from1865 onwards on a regular, permanent basis. This was a highly significant achievement.

Another important milestone was reached when Emily was asked - the first woman ever to be asked - to give evidence to a Royal Commission set up to look at conditions in schools. At first the enquiry was limited to boys' schools but Emily succeeded in convincing the Commissioners to extend their remit to girls' schools. The Commission's eventual report fully vindicated her views that girls' schools were in desperate need of improvement both in buildings and in the quality of education.

Many of Emily's ideas at this time were formalised in her book *The Higher Education of Women* published in 1866.

Despite some progress, universities remained stubbornly resistant to the idea of women studying on anything remotely like the same terms as men. The most they would consider were courses and examinations of a lower standard, something that was anathema to Emily and led her to conceive her great plan of establishing her own women's college. She was, however, persuaded to put this idea on temporary hold, in 1866, to support her friend Barbara Bodichon and others in the campaign for votes for women. In that year, John Stuart Mill, the philosopher, was elected to Parliament on a platform of supporting women's suffrage. To further this cause, Emily and Barbara asked if he would present a petition to Parliament. He agreed on condition that they could collect at least a hundred signatures - Emily promptly collected 1,500! However Mills' attempt to bring in a women's suffrage bill failed - possibly because he insisted that all women should have the vote straight away which, in Emily's view, was right in principle but was tactically unwise, given that Parliament had only ever widened the male franchise in small stages.

After this setback, Emily returned with renewed vigour to her plans for a women's college. Given her previous work on the Cambridge Local Examinations she felt that a link to Cambridge would be best. Again the obstacles were considerable and she frequently encountered ludicrous arguments as to why women should be denied higher education. It was claimed that learning would make them masculine and that they would no longer be good wives, mothers or sisters. It was claimed that they were not physically strong enough to study - an argument that Emily, having seen the hard labour undertaken by Gateshead women workers, found grotesque. With unbounded energy, she argued and cajoled to win support and to change some of these entrenched views.

By 1869 Emily had raised funds and acquired a building - Benslow House in Hitchin - and established a College Committee and appointed a mistress. She also engaged sympathetic Cambridge dons as lecturers for the five pioneering women students of the first intake to ensure that the teaching was exactly of the same standard as that offered to Cambridge men. Three years later the College moved to new, purpose-built accommodation in Girton - a village only three miles from Cambridge - and from that time onwards Girton College, Cambridge, went gradually but purposefully from strength to strength, establishing a reputation for learning at the highest level.

Emily, not having had a formal education, did not teach the students herself. Her genius lay in planning, organising, and persuading. She was totally focussed on achieving her goals and inspired her students who knew that responsibility rested with them to show how much women, once admitted to an academic environment, could achieve. It is also striking how many of the early intakes of students returned to the College to teach and to help it further enhance its performance and reputation.

While frustrations and difficulties continued - for example women did not become full members of the University until 1948! - the excellence of Girton's standards were clear for all to see. It was, indeed, the trailblazer for women's higher education throughout the country.

Emily retired from Girton at the age of seventy-four in 1904 but her active public life was not yet over. The campaign for women's suffrage had taken on new momentum and Emily wanted to play her part. Within a year of leaving Girton, she had managed to bring together the various and disparate suffrage societies together into one central organisation - a huge achievement in a short time and one that would make the overall movement more effective. However both Emily and Millicent Garrett Fawcett were on the side of those who rejected violent militancy, which they felt would alienate government and give opponents of women's suffrage an excuse to refuse to give way. Indeed Lloyd George refused to meet Emily and Millie 'on account of militancy' somewhat proving their point! Arguments take place to this day over whether militants or moderates were right. In the end the clinching circumstance that won women the vote was probably the key roles that women played in the First World War so that by the end of that appalling conflict the granting of the vote was inevitable and the long pro-suffrage campaigns were finally victorious.

It is richly gratifying, that after a lifetime of support for women's votes Emily herself lived long enough to cast her vote at the 1919 post-war election at the age of eighty-eight. However, it is her pioneering work for women's higher education that is her lasting legacy and today's university educated women, just as much as their predecessors, have every reason to honour her memory.

Besides the plaque commemorating her in Gateshead there are plaques in Southampton (where she was born) and in St John's Wood, London where she moved to in 1860. Commemorative tablets are also to be found at Benslow House in Hitchin (now a Care Home) and, naturally, at Girton itself. In addition there is the delightful College portrait of her by Rudolph Lehmann.

Emily Wilding Davison (1872-1913)

Leading Suffragette and Campaigner

'Fight the Good Fight'

Emily Wilding Davison.

Emily Wilding Davison would have been proud to be labelled a 'militant' suffragette. Her death when she ran in front of the King's Horse at the Epsom Derby in June 1913 waving the suffragette flag has, however, been the subject of speculation and controversy ever since. Was she deliberately committing suicide to become a martyr or was her death the result of a demonstration for the cause she held so dear that simply went disastrously wrong?

That she was prepared to die for the suffragette cause cannot be in doubt.

She had previously risked her life on a number of occasions. However, the claim that she was deliberately committing suicide on that Derby Day in 1913 does not stand up to scrutiny. She had a return rail ticket in her pocket, she was looking forward to taking part in further meetings and demonstrations, and what is known about her life and character all seem to back up the theory that on this particular occasion the risks to her survival that she was always prepared to take ended, accidentally, in tragedy.

Today Emily is firmly associated with Northumberland - both with Morpeth, where she is buried in St Mary's Churchyard, and with the village of Longhorsley where her mother lived and ran a shop. During the height of her suffragette activities it was to Northumberland that Emily frequently returned both to see her mother, to whom she was very close, and to relax and to recover her strength and energy for further militant engagement.

Emily's family roots were in Northumberland. Descended from a family originally from Wooler, her father belonged to Morpeth and her mother to nearby Longhirst. However, Emily herself was born in Blackheath and spent her childhood in London and the Home Counties. She was the child of a second family as her father, Charles Edward Davison, was a widower with nine children at the time of his marriage to Emily's mother, Margaret, who then bore him three more children of whom Emily was the middle one, having an older brother and a younger sister. The large family - despite the age gap between the two sets of siblings - was by all accounts happy and the parents were keen that all the children should experience the benefits of education. Emily was a pupil at Kensington High School and then, after passing the Oxford and Cambridge Higher School Certificate, attended Holloway College, ironically not far from Holloway Women's prison which she would later in her life get to know all too well.

While at Holloway College Emily's circumstances changed dramatically as her father died suddenly, leaving little money to his large family and prompting Emily's mother to move back to Longhorsley in Northumberland to try to make ends meet. Emily got a post as a governess, but managed to complete her studies at the same time with spectacular effect, being awarded a First Class Degree in English Language and Literature. She then embarked on a teaching career, and over the next sixteen years taught at state and private schools, followed by a happy period of six years as resident governess and tutor in a private household.

Emily first joined the Women's Social and Political Union in 1906, aged thirty-three. This was at a time when the Suffrage movement was becoming increasingly frustrated at the lack of progress after so many years of campaigning. Her involvement quickly grew and after eighteen months she became an officer of the Union. At this point she made a decision to become a full-time campaigner and to spend her time helping to organise protests and write articles. She fully supported the move to greater militancy, believing that non-militant methods had failed.

Over the next seven years, Emily's participation in protests and demonstrations led to her being imprisoned on several occasions and in different gaols around the country - Holloway, London; Strangeways, Manchester; Aberdeen; Liverpool and Winson Green, Birmingham. She demonstrated in towns and cities throughout the land, including in Newcastle, and spoke at many rallies and meetings throughout the country. She often addressed meetings in the North East, where she had close links with many of the local suffragette societies and their members.

The militant activity of the movement began with such activities as women chaining themselves to railings at prominent government sites and progressed to others such as smashing windows, starting fires, and even planting primitive bombing devices. The aim was to disrupt and to damage property - and therefore gain publicity and attention - but without harming people. The only known example of Emily assaulting a person was the strange episode in Aberdeen when she was found guilty of attempting to horsewhip a Baptist Minister whom, allegedly, she mistook for the Chancellor of the Exchequer, David Lloyd-George, whom the suffragettes particularly condemned for his betrayal of his early pro-suffrage views. Yet, as Emily's biographers, Liz Stanley and Ann Morley, point out, that incident is shrouded with uncertainty and seems out of character with the rest of Emily's campaigning exploits.

Prison sentences were often the result of repeated offences or refusals to pay fines for 'offences' and actions that Emily and her fellow campaigners felt were fully justified. When in prison she and others frequently resorted to hunger strikes in protest at the refusal of the authorities to treat them as political prisoners. Hunger strikes eventually led to the notorious practice of force-feeding whereby the women were held down, their mouths or noses prised open and rubber tubes passed down their throats. Emily described graphically the torture she endured on these occasions but consistently refused to cooperate merely to secure her own relief or release. On one occasion in Holloway, in protest against her treatment and that of her fellow victims she threw herself from a railing on to a staircase feeling that by doing so - even if she were horribly injured or killed - she might save others from being subjected to similar degradation.

Not surprisingly, the House of Commons itself was a focus of many suffragette demonstrations and protests. Emily broke into Parliament on at least three occasions most memorably on the night of the 1911 Census. The suffragettes were refusing to fill in Census papers in protest against their disenfranchisement and Emily hid in the cupboard at the back of the Crypt of St. Stephen's Chapel to avoid being registered. She was discovered, but ironically, since she was in Parliament at the time of the Census - and given that the address which had to be supplied to the Census was where you happened to be at the time of registration - her address was recorded as the House of Commons, the first woman to whom that had ever applied!

Before that fateful day in Epsom in 1913 Emily had fully earned her spurs for the suffragette cause. How many of her activities were sanctioned by the Suffragette leaders however is not clear. Emily and others often acted alone - not wanting to implicate their fellow campaigners by their actions and perhaps not wanting to be bound by the decisions of some of the Suffragette leaders, including the Pankhursts. Because of this independence of action some critics have characterised Emily as an eccentric loner. The evidence for this however is contradicted by the large number of friends she had in the movement and outside. Within the movement she seems to have been particularly close to Mary Leigh, Mary Richardson, Dora Marston, Rose Lamartine Yeats, Edith Mansell-Moullin, Elinor Penn-Gaskell and 'Miss' Morrison.

Emily's closeness to her mother was well known to the villagers of Longhorsley, as was her love of the Northumbrian countryside. In his book about Emily, published in 1988, John Sleight talked to a number of local people who had met her or who knew people who had met her. Many remembered her liveliness, her energy, her talented piano playing, and her concern for children as well as her strong views. Some decried her as the 'lawless lassie', others remembered her with affection as a 'favourite aunt'.

A charming incident, indicative of her love of children is the memory of her distributing black

DAILY SKETCH.

HISTORY'S MOST WONDERFUL DERBY; FIRST HORSE DISQUALIFIED; A 100 TO 1 CHANCE WINS; SUFFRAGETTE NEARLY KILLED BY THE KING'S COLT.

In Memoriam.

Miss Emily Wilding Davison, B.A.

Top) The *Daily Sketch* on the 5th June 1913. Above) A memorial leaflet from 1913. Right) On 14 June 1913 Davison's body was transported from Epsom to London; her coffin was inscribed 'Fight on. God will give the victory.' The procession stopped at St George's, Bloomsbury for a brief service - shown here, then the coffin was transported by train to Newcastle, then to be interred at Morpeth.

bullets - those well-loved Northern sweets - from her mother's shop to local youngsters in celebration of her success in obtaining her degree. She took pleasure in many things while maintaining her political and religious convictions, being throughout her life a committed, practising Christian.

After her injuries at Epsom, Emily languished four days, unconscious, before dying on June 8th 1913. Her funeral a week later attracted vast crowds, unprecedented for someone who was not royalty - and a woman at that! It was a huge demonstration of support for the suffragette movement although Emmeline Pankhurst herself was not able to be present having been arrested en route! The scenes at Morpeth, whence Emily's coffin was brought by train, were equally extraordinary with so many women wanting to be present that an extra train carriage was added at Newcastle. There were over 200 floral tributes and some 20,000 people lined the route in Morpeth from the station to the churchyard.

As well as Emily's grave in Morpeth, there is a plaque adorning the shop and home in Longhorsley. There is also a plaque in the House of Commons cupboard where Emily hid on Census night. Interest in Emily's life was rekindled at the time of the centenary of her death in 2013 and continues as, for example, in the film *Suffragette* released in 2015.

Ruth Dodds (1890-1976)

Writer, Politician and Founder of Gateshead's Little Theatre

The three sisters, Sylvia, Hope and Ruth, 1917.

In paying tribute to the work of Ruth Dodds, it is important to recognise the contribution of her two sisters Hope (1885-1972) and Sylvia (1892-1969), since they were both closely involved with Ruth's work and also made their own mark in a number of ways.

Ruth was the fourth child of Edwin and Emily Bryham Dodds. She had two elder sisters Molly and Madeleine (Hope), and a brother, Brian. Her younger sister Sylvia was just under two years her junior. Together with Hope and Sylvia, Ruth lived all her life (apart from some periods of education) in the family home, Home House in Low Fell.

The family was well to do and father, Edwin, owned and ran a local printing and bookbinding business. They were also related to other prominent local families. Joseph Swan, the great inventor was Ruth's great-uncle and her maternal grandfather was John Mawson, of the well-known Tyneside firm Mawson, Swan and Morgan. Both Mawson and Swan were neighbours of the Dodds family in Low Fell.

Education for girls as well as boys was considered important in the family. Ruth attended Gateshead High School for Girls until she was fifteen and then went to Clapham High School to finish her education. Her sister Hope went on to higher education at Newnham College Cambridge, studying history there and attaining an honours degree in history (although women were not entitled formally to be granted degrees at the time)!

Typically for unmarried daughters in well-off families the three girls Ruth, Hope and Sylvia do not seem to have been expected to have to seek regular long-term employment. Less typically however they seem to have all been motivated towards public service and engagement in the wider community in different ways.

The three girls were all keenly interested in literature, the theatre and the study of history. Ruth together with Hope authored a book, *The Pilgrimage of Grace* in 1915, which, for a hundred years, was the principal historical account of the Northern Rebellion in 1536 against Henry VIII's break with Rome, his imposition of new taxes and his dissolution of the monasteries. Hope edited volumes of the County History of Northumberland and for a number of years was librarian to the Newcastle Society of Antiquaries.

In the First World War Ruth worked for a time in Armstrong's munitions factory on Tyneside, a period of life described vividly in her diaries. She describes the attractive but flimsy cotton garments the women workers wore - garments which would horrify today's Health and Safety inspectors. The conditions were difficult, the hours long, and numerous accidents occurred. Her experiences of war work and the knowledge she gained of some of the harsh circumstances of her fellow-workers may also help to explain why, during the period of the War from 1915 onwards she became interested in politics.

From a Liberal background she became increasingly drawn towards socialism, joining the Independent Labour Party. Her first official public speaking engagement was in 1919 when she was asked to chair a meeting of the ILP in the absence of Dr Ethel Williams. Ruth was also active in the suffrage movement and became the secretary of the Gateshead branch of the National Union of Women's Suffrage Societies.

Her political involvement deepened during the 1920s. She worked for her brother in the family business but left after disagreements with him about the 1926 General Strike and the role of Trade Unions. When the ILP disaffiliated from the Labour Party, Ruth joined the Socialist League, which favoured continued affiliation, and she became the League's Regional Representative on its National Council. Ruth edited Gateshead Labour News and Labour Herald. She opposed Ramsay MacDonald's 'National Government'. She and Hope helped with the purchase of Westfield Hall as premises for the Independent Labour Party and for the Labour Party itself and this building became a de facto regional Labour Party headquarters.

In 1929 Ruth was elected to Gateshead Council and during her term of office opened four new welfare clinics for children. She was deeply concerned for the welfare of the town's children and their mothers, many of whom were living in slum conditions in the 1920s and 30s. Also during the 1930s Ruth was involved in fundraising for the victims of the Spanish Civil War and in helping refugees from Austria and Czechoslovakia, providing hostel accommodation and assistance in resettling. Ruth was interested in standing for Parliament but failed to be selected in 1931 and 1936.

Having been a significant Labour figure in the town, as a convinced pacifist she resigned from the Labour Party in 1939 because of its support for war. However, her diaries reveal that pacifism in 1939 was not as straightforward a choice for her as it was in the very different circumstances of the First World War. She wrote; 'Feeling as I do a half-sympathy with a war against fascism is it really honest for me to say that my pacifism makes me resign? Is it just because I said I would resign if and when the Party supported a war?' This was obviously a difficult time for her and although she rejoined Labour after the war she would no longer be as actively involved politically as previously.

Although politics was a key part of Ruth's life it is in the world of theatre and culture that her legacy - and that of her sisters - lives on. She was active from the outset in the 'Progressive Players', the dramatic club of the Independent Labour Party. In 1923 she produced *The Pitman's Pay* - a drama about Thomas Hepburn, the miners' leader and creator of the first Miners'

Union in 1825. The inspiration for her play was the poem *The Pitman's Pay* by Thomas Wilson of Gateshead, and written around 1826-30. The poem had been widely read at the time and Ruth's play, in its turn, enjoyed success and national recognition. It was enacted in many villages in the North East, particularly during the General Strike. Ruth and her sisters were also involved in - and supportive of - the Newcastle Criterion Players and the People's Theatre. However it is with the establishment of the Little Theatre in Gateshead that her name, along with her sister Hope in particular, is most closely linked. Surprisingly this was built in the early years of the Second World War (the only new theatre in Britain to be built at that time) although negotiations to acquire the site for a theatre had taken place sometime before. During the war the theatre hosted the North East Regional Drama Festival, which involved Ruth staging twenty-one different plays in six days! To celebrate the Theatre's first anniversary Hope, a devoted Jane Austen fan, wrote a stage adaptation of *Emma* - the theatre's seventh production.

The Little Theatre thrived and became a permanent and well-loved part of the North East's cultural scene, but its origins, as the plaque commemorating Ruth and her sisters in Gateshead makes clear, are entirely due to the vision and generosity of Ruth and her sisters, and those local people who supported them. Indeed Ruth continued to act until her seventies and remained passionate about the theatre and its contribution to local culture. In 1966, in recognition of her outstanding contribution to the town, Ruth was made a Freeman of the Borough of Gateshead, the first woman to be so honoured. Her diary describes this occasion in the words 'A lovely day and all went off splendidly. I had a new dress made for the occasion. Hope was on the platform with me. Lots of old friends. Sylvia of course looking very smart and imposing'.

Ruth's diaries, which span a total of sixty-nine years from 1905 until 1974, and which were published by Maureen Calcott in 1995 are a fascinating read. Her compelling descriptions of life for women in the First World War have - at a time when we have commemorated the centenary of that conflict - rightly won her new readers and admirers. Overall the diaries reveal an intelligent, energetic, highly motivated and compassionate woman. She analyses her own feelings and motivations openly, yet not obsessively but rather more in the vein of giving herself occasionally a good talking to. What is conveyed is her enjoyment in the company of family and friends, her attachment to home and well-loved places and her fondness for travelling. She also comes across as someone combining keen intellectual curiosity with strong convictions.

Ruth died in 1976 aged eighty-six. Her sisters Hope and Sylvia predeceased her by a few years. She and they will continue to be remembered in their home town of Gateshead but they are worthy of being remembered more widely.

Elizabeth Elstob's self
portrait from her
English-Saxon homily
on the birth-day of
St. Gregory (1709).

Elizabeth Elstob
(1683-1756)

Anglo-Saxon Scholar

Elizabeth Elstob was a pioneer of medieval studies at a time when it was a neglected branch of learning. She was the first female Anglo-Saxon scholar and the first person to publish a Grammar of Old English written in modern English. She is now widely acknowledged as an exceptional intellect, a talented linguist and an excellent scholar. Her vehement insistence on education for women was centuries ahead of her time and today she is considered one of Britain's earliest feminists, along with her fellow 'geordie', Mary Astell. Sadly, her life story provides an example of the catastrophic effect of the constraints and prejudices women suffered in the eighteenth century.

The prevailing reality was a patriarchal society based around the family. Women were seen as weaker vessels with smaller brains, more emotional and less rational than men. They were defined by their capacity to bear children and were expected to confine themselves to the male-defined 'domestic sphere'. Middle-class boys received their education in schools and universities or in some other form of training to prepare them for a profession. Girls remained at home, sometimes with a governess, tutored just enough to prepare them for marriage and motherhood.

The Elstob family were squires in Foxton near Sedgefield in County Durham for hundreds of years, although Elizabeth's father, Ralph Elstob, a younger son, established himself as a merchant on the Quayside in Newcastle and it was in Newcastle that Elizabeth and William her elder brother were born and raised. Their father became Sheriff of Newcastle in 1686 -1687, but he died a year later, leaving his family ill-provided for. Their mother died only four years later and although Elizabeth was only eight years old, she remembered her mother as a great lover of books who encouraged the desire for learning in her children.

Their uncle, Dr Charles Elstob, prebendary of Canterbury Cathedral was appointed guardian and Elizabeth was sent to live with him in Canterbury. In 1697 they moved to Tillington in Sussex. William was destined for the Church and went from Eton to study at Queen's College Cambridge and University College, Oxford. At the time these colleges were the main centres for Anglo-Saxon studies. William duly entered the Anglican priesthood and in 1705 became a Doctor of Divinity. In 1702 he was appointed to the joint parishes of St Swithin and St Mary Bothaw in the City of London, with an annual income of £140. While he did not neglect his parochial responsibilities, during the brief course of his life William Elstob established himself as a brilliant Anglo-Saxon Scholar.

Elizabeth was ten years younger than her brother and, like him, brilliant with a passionate love of learning. Her guardian, Dr Charles, however, had a very conservative view of women's education; it is recorded that he 'disdained it', believing that, 'one tongue is enough for a woman'. William had a much more liberal view and, despite his guardian, encouraged Elizabeth and tutored her when he could. Elizabeth learned both Latin and French as a child despite being denied the benefits of formal schooling.

While her brother was at University, Elizabeth stayed with him whenever she could. In 1702 she escaped the restrictions of her uncle's household and went to live with William in his parish in London, as his companion and housekeeper. From then onwards they each supported the other in their scholarly interests and their household became something of a centre for Saxon scholars with whom Elizabeth mingled freely.

Living in London opened many doors for Elizabeth. From 1702 she became part of the circle of intellectual women around Mary Astell. William was a founder member of what was to become the Society of Antiquaries in London.

Elizabeth was prompted to learn Old English to gain access to primary sources in her medieval studies. She was the first woman ever to learn Early English. She claimed that her childhood in the North of England, her familiarity with its dialects and accents made it easier for her to grasp the language quickly. In all Elizabeth became proficient in eight languages.

Elizabeth's first publication was a translation from French into English of an essay by the seventeenth century French scholar, Madeleine de Scudery. Her first major Anglo-Saxon work was published in 1709. This was a translation into modern English of Abbot Aelfric of Eynsham's tenth century *An English-Saxon Homily on the Birth-Day of St Gregory*. The text was important because it had been preached regularly throughout the Anglo-Saxon period and described the life of Pope Gregory, and the Conversion of the English from Paganism to Christianity.

Elizabeth's edition was complex and she spent extravagantly on it. There are several lovely engravings, one of which is Elizabeth's self-portrait. There is an eight-page dedication to Queen Anne, followed by a sixty page preface in which Elizabeth ventures into controversial religious and political issues, subjects considered then to be out of bounds to women. The preface is followed by forty-five pages of the homily itself, though most of the pages are taken up with extensive notes on the contentious issues she raises in the preface. The final sections of the book are her brother's Latin translation of the homily, and an appendix of all Gregory's letters.

Among the controversial issues Elizabeth raises are arguments against slavery. She cites Pope Gregory who freed slaves and set them up in the monasteries he had established. She argues passionately for the restoration to the Anglican Church of the simple purity of the Anglo-Saxon church, she discusses the various doctrinal issues raised at the Synod of Whitby, and she argues vehemently for women's right to education using religious ideas to support her case. Elizabeth wrote: 'If women may be said to have Souls, and if good learning be one of the Soul's greatest improvements ... What is the fault in Women seeking after learning?' She goes on to cite the achievements of Anna Maria van Schurman, 1607- 1678, the first female university student, a Dutch painter, poet and scholar known for her exceptional learning.

268 subscribers supported the publication of the English-Saxon Homily. They included aristocrats, antiquarians and 116 women, and, because she retained her Northern connections, twenty-four were well-known inhabitants of Newcastle, including the Mayor and four Aldermen.

The work demonstrates her command of Greek, Latin, Old English and French and was widely acknowledged as being of great scholarship, however one medievalist, Thomas Hearne, objected to her explanatory notes just because they involved religious and political issues, subjects considered taboo for women. He called the work a 'Ferrago of Vanities,' and then hysterically alleged that her brother must be the real author! Hearne's views were completely spurious and are mentioned only to demonstrate the hostility that female scholars suffered at the time.

Elizabeth Elstob's second major work was, *The Rudiments of Grammar for the English Saxon Tongue*. Published in 1715, it was the first grammar written in English, not Latin and remains, after three hundred years, one of the very few such works to be published by a woman. She wrote it in English specifically so that it would be accessible to other English women, who would have had no Latin. It enjoyed a very wide circulation. Thomas Jefferson, third President of the United States, a keen linguist and lawyer, owned a copy. While today scholars recognise the elegance and attractiveness of the work and praise its erudition, some contemporary male writers scorned the work of a so-called, 'Petticoat Author'!

By the year 1715 Elizabeth had already begun another ambitious piece of scholarship; the translation and publication of all seventeen of Aelfric's Catholic Homilies. But tragedy struck. William, her brother, closest friend and her lifelong mentor, died aged forty-two. Elizabeth was just thirty-two and coming into her prime, and yet her scholarly career was over. She never again tackled another Anglo Saxon Project.

William's death left Elizabeth without a home, penniless, and without any means of support but with the mountain of debts they had incurred in financing their expensive publications. In desperation she opened a girl's school in Chelsea, but within six months it had failed. In 1718 she fled London and her creditors, leaving behind all her books and the partial manuscript of the Homilies (now preserved at the British Library) and simply disappeared.

Seventeen years were to pass before her friends discovered her whereabouts. She had hidden herself away in rural Worcester under the assumed name of Frances Smith. She was living in penury while running a small Dame School. Her friends came to her help and in 1738 she was introduced to Margaret Bentinck, Duchess of Portland, who appointed her governess to her children. Elizabeth Elstob, the brilliant scholar, remained merely a children's governess at Bulstrode Park, Buckinghamshire until her death in 1756, aged seventy-three. Embittered by her predicament she wrote near the end of her life, 'This is not an Age to hope for any encouragement to learning of any kind.' She is buried in the churchyard of St Margaret's, Westminster.

Elizabeth's life story illustrates perfectly that women in the eighteenth century (as now) could be as accomplished in scholarship as men. What women lacked was not ability or strength but education and opportunity. As things were, without either a male mentor or independent means, women could not become scholars. Very few opportunities existed for them. They could not be ordained (the church had provided an income for William, who in turn had supported his sister) there was no place in politics for women, they could not become members of a college and the professions were closed to them. As we have seen, Elizabeth Elstob's primary concern was Anglo-Saxon studies, to which she made a pioneering contribution. Her beautiful books are her legacy and her work continues to inspire young medievalists today. There are modern editions of some of her writings currently available.

Elizabeth Elstob was also one of the very first British feminists. Not only was she adamant and outspoken about the need for women's education but her very deliberate public forays into matters of doctrine and politics in the prefaces and notes of her books were exceptionally radical for a woman in the eighteenth century.

Lady Sybil Grey OBE (1882-1966)

Established the Red Cross Hospital in Petrograd 1916

This brief account of the achievements of Lady Sybil Grey during the First World War is only one testament to the flood of patriotism that swept the country throughout the war period. Women from every strata of British Society made a huge contribution to the war effort and for those women born into the gilded circle of the aristocracy there was the added expectation that they would assume leadership roles. From the outset Lady Sybil's commitment was total and it was with cheerfulness and a can-do attitude that the young Lady Sybil Grey bravely shouldered several leadership roles between 1914 and 1920.

Lady Sybil was the second daughter of Albert Henry George Grey, Fourth Earl Grey 1851-1917, whose family seat is Howick Hall in Northumberland. He served as Administrator of Rhodesia and Governor General of Canada. Sybil's cousin, Sir Edward Grey, was Foreign Secretary at the outbreak of the War, (1905 to 1916). Lady Sybil and her sisters were educated privately at home in Northumberland. She was a clever, sociable, confident and adventurous child and enjoyed horse riding, sport and fishing. The family were widely

Boyd Family Collection

Sybil Grey in the uniform of the Women's Legion.

travelled. Lady Sybil lived in Canada for seven years, visited Europe and Africa, and in early 1914 travelled round the world with her parents.

Lady Sybil showed great initiative in the first year of the war, caring for recovering wounded soldiers. When war broke out there was a chronic shortage of medical personnel, particularly nurses. Lady Sybil Grey was quick off the blocks and as early as October 1914 had completed her training as a nursing assistant on the Men's Surgical Ward at Newcastle Infirmary, thus joining the thousands of women in Voluntary Aid Detachments up and down the country.

The nationwide shortage of hospital beds was resolved by establishing Voluntary Aid Auxiliary (or convalescent) Hospitals in stately homes. The Grey family was first in Northumberland to volunteer their home, and by October 1914, Sybil, her mother the Countess Alice and Lady Mabel Grey, had converted one wing of Howick Hall into a thirty-one bed VAD Hospital. (During the course of the war, eighteen such hospitals were established in Northumberland). After only a few months Sybil became the hospital Commandant. Medical staff were appointed, led by a fully trained nursing sister, and included an honorary medical officer, a dentist, a masseuse (physiotherapist) and VADs drawn from Alnmouth, Ellingham and Alnwick. During its brief life this hospital treated 411 wounded soldiers, officers and men, British, French and Belgian. The hospital closed in January 1916, because Lady Sybil was called to serve in Russia and the Countess's role as President of the Northumberland Red Cross made it impossible for her to continue working there.

Lady Sybil was asked by the philanthropist Lady Muriel Paget to establish and run a 200-bed Anglo-Russian Red Cross Hospital in Petrograd, the capital of Tsarist Russia. The Russians were suffering horrendous casualties and the hospital was meant as a goodwill gesture from the British and was funded largely by public subscription. It was a mammoth undertaking by any standards, and the British Journal of Nursing did object to the idea of Sybil's leadership of this huge project, describing her as, 'a young and inexperienced girl'. It is true that she was just thirty-three years old and had only three weeks' medical training and less than two years' nursing experience, however an experienced medical team had already been appointed and Sybil's role was not medical. Her task was to win the help and support of members of the Russian elite and Embassy officials using her fluent French, the preferred foreign language of the Russian court. She was lively, attractive, well connected and able to interact socially with Russian high society. She had considerable organisational skills and was thought unflappable. For these reasons she was a good choice. Sybil was well aware of the dangers. She knew that Tsarist Russia was in turmoil due to food shortages, political intrigue and heavy military losses. The Lusitania had been torpedoed by the Germans only months earlier and the journey to Russia would involve two days crossing the

North Sea, followed by an overland journey of over 2000 miles. Knowing all this Sybil bravely accepted the challenge though not without some trepidation. Throughout her travels Sybil kept a diary and wrote regular letters home. This correspondence provides an excellent account of her work and that of her colleagues and the hospital. Having once decided to go, she moved quickly and by mid-October 1915 the advance party arrived in Petrograd. It was a particularly cold winter and they had to set about finding premises, adapting and equipping them to create a 200-bed hospital with accommodation for thirty medical staff. They found that just about every public building had already been converted into hospitals as there were already so many in the city. Astonishingly, after only three months, and with the help of the British Embassy and the Russian Red Cross, the hospital was opened by the Tsarina, on the ground floor of the Dimitri Palace in February 1916. The wounded flooded in.

The hospital organisation and services were excellent, indeed the pioneering neuro-surgeon Geoffrey Jefferson served there for eighteen months. Once the main hospital was up and running, and because it was hundreds of miles away from the battle front, Lady Paget and Lady Sybil decided to assemble the equipment for Field Hospitals, which could be moved to within a few miles of the firing line. Lady Sybil volunteered to establish the first of these. Leaving Lady Paget in control in June 1916, she set out on the long journey to the Russian Front. Her Red Cross train carried tents, medical supplies and equipment, horses, carts and ambulances, kitchens on wheels, water boilers and barrels. With her were nineteen medical staff, interpreters and orderlies. The actual site of the field hospital changed from time to time depending on where the action was and always involved negotiation with the Russian army because the front was 400 kilometres long. At first the base was established at Veropoeva, twenty-eight kilometres from the front, with a casualty station at Postaviin just behind the firing line. Lady Sybil and her party endured hardship and adventure during the process of placing the Field Hospital and ancillary casualty stations, travelling sometimes on horseback, camping out, and sleeping in empty buildings, fortunately things which Sybil seemed to enjoy, and wrote home about with great humour.

On July 1 1916, while watching a demonstration of hand grenade practice by the Russian army, near Molodechna, Sybil was seriously injured when shrapnel entered her left cheek and lodged in her skull. She was sent back to Petrograd to have the shrapnel removed and returned home to recuperate. Despite the seriousness of her injury she was back at her post by October 1916.

In December Rasputin was murdered and by January 1917 Tsar Nicholas had lost control of the situation. There were horrendous numbers of Russian war casualties, a desperate refugee crisis and terrible fuel and food shortages, and in

February 1917 the first of the two Russian revolutions occurred. There was chaos and violence all around, and Sybil even had to face down a mob which invaded the hospital. Under her leadership the staff remained at their posts throughout terrifying times but clearly things could not continue as before. As fate would have it, in the summer of 1917 Lady Sybil received news that her father was dying of stomach cancer and so she left Russia to be with him. Fortunately this also meant she avoided the Russian Revolution of October 1917. Earl Grey died in August 1917. The Anglo Russian Hospital had to be closed in early 1918 and the staff safely repatriated. This was the end of the most challenging episode of Sybil's life.

After only the shortest of interludes, in February 1918 Lady Sybil became commandant of the Astley Hospital for officers based in the magnificent Dorchester House on Park Lane. Always looking for a challenge, in the summer of 1919 she was off again to Wimereux near Calais, having successfully applied for the Command of the Women's Legion in France.

It is strange to think that her first experience of wearing a military uniform came when the war was over. The Women's Legion was founded in 1915 by the Marchioness of Londonderry, at its height there were 40,000 members. When Sybil took over the French section there were over 500 members scattered across administrative areas in northern France and Belgium, mostly in the motor transport section. Although the war was over there was still convoy work, ambulance duties and chauffeuring to do, though Sybil's main task was to ensure the orderly demobilisation of the Women's Legion and their safe return to England. Once again she discharged her duties with distinction. Brigadier General E. Gibb wrote as much to the War Office. The work was completed by April 1920 and Sybil returned home for a very well-deserved rest. For Lady Sybil Grey the war was over, she was thirty-eight years old and had served her country with distinction and bravery.

In 1919 Lady Sybil Grey was awarded the OBE for her services to the Voluntary Aid Hospital at Howick. She, along with Lady Muriel Paget, is known as the driving force behind the establishment of the Anglo-Russian Hospital in Petrograd. Until recently the hospital has been largely forgotten despite its capacity to treat more than 4,000 wounded Russian troops over its two-year existence, and it actually treated many more soldiers in its field hospitals.

In 1922 Lady Sybil was married in the chapel on the Howick estate and went on to live a happily married life. She had two children and with her husband, Lambert Middleton and travelled widely until his death in 1941. Lady Sybil lived for a further twenty-five years and died after a short illness in 1966, aged eighty-four. She was buried in Hampshire. There are no memorials to her.

Isa (Isabella) Jobling (1851-1926)

Landscape and genre painter in oil and watercolour

Isabella Thompson enjoyed a genteel upbringing in Newcastle. She was the fourth daughter and fifth child of Mark Thompson, an ambitious ships' chandler with business premises on the Quayside. At the time of her birth the family lived in a pleasant terrace house in Cumberland Row on the west side of the city but as business improved they moved in 1860 to Graingerville, an impressive elegant terrace at the top of the hill to the west and further away from the industrial grime of the City (near the present General Hospital). The family had two servants.

In her teens, Isa attended the Newcastle School of Design and afterwards her father sent her to Paris to study art. Little is known of her work or her movements immediately after her return from Paris, but her father died in 1875 and in the early 1880s Isa, a single lady, moved into lodgings in Cullercoats, eventually settling in Victoria Terrace on the sea front. She moved into what was in effect an artists' colony. Cullercoats in the 1880s was still a quaint fishing village with huge pictorial possibilities, (first discovered by John Wilson Carmichael in the 1820s) and in which a number of aspiring artists, including Robert Jobling, John Surtees and Henry Hetherington Emmerson were living. Isa was unusual among aspiring women artists in that she had no patron and no husband, and by then her father was dead. She was quite alone and so the move to Cullercoats meant that she was surrounded by like-minded people. This energised her and gave her moral support.

The period was one of rapid industrialisation throughout the country, with its attendant overcrowding, disease and hardship. The Cullercoats artists recoiled from all that and took solace in depicting rural idylls, painting poetic visions of the sea and romanticising the lives of the fisher folk at the seaside, creating images the Victorians loved. This genre became the focus of Isa's work and she excelled at it and from the 1880s began to make her mark. She first exhibited her work in 1883 and by 1887, the year of Queen Victoria's Jubilee Exhibition at the Bewick Club, she was showing works of distinguished merit, beautiful compositions with well drawn figures and charming and effective use of light and colour. Two excellent paintings are *Fortune Telling* and *Storms be Sudden*. The first shows a young fishwife predicting the future lives and loves of her companions with a pack of cards. It portrays a group of six young women, brilliantly highlighting the camaraderie between them and their enjoyment of each other. *Storms be Sudden*, depicts a comely, strong young mother and her child, battling the winds blowing along the seashore.

In 1889 she moved from Cullercoats and took lodgings in 6 Wentworth terrace off Elswick Road, in Newcastle, she also established her own studio in Market Street. She had already begun to visit the now famous North Yorkshire village of Staithes and her huge and ambitious exhibit *Fisher Folk,* depicting Staithes' fisherwomen was shown at the Royal Academy and at the Walker Art Gallery in Liverpool in 1893. She was forty and had just begun to go places, finding her way onto the mainstream exhibition circuit of Victorian artists. During the ten years from 1883 to 1893, Isa Thompson exhibited around forty paintings, at the Royal Academy, the Scottish Academy, the Bewick Club and the Suffolk Street Gallery in London.

However Isa's life changed considerably when in 1893 she married Robert Jobling, ten years her senior and recently widowed with five children, three of whom were still living at home. Their home was 29, Victoria Avenue, overlooking the sea near Cullercoats. Robert Jobling was already a leading light in the art world of the North East. By his own efforts he had risen from being a ships' painter at the Tyne General Ferry Yard in the St Peter's district of Newcastle, to Vice president of the influential Bewick Art Club. He enjoyed a huge network of male contacts and the patronage of several important local figures including Charles Mitchell one of the Newcastle's most powerful

Isa Thompson with her
artist's materials -
possibily at her
Market Street studio.

industrial magnates. Robert Jobling had already been exhibiting paintings successfully for twenty-seven years when he and Isa married.

It was clear from the outset that theirs could never be a marriage of equally important artists - that was not the Victorian way. He was the established artist and she his wife and helpmate. She was forty-one years old and understood this and willingly embraced her new role. So while he continued to work from his studio in Newcastle she gave hers up and worked, whenever her domestic duties allowed, in a lean-to glazed studio off the back room of their house. After her marriage, as expected she signed her work Isa Jobling. Isa undoubtedly found a great deal of personal happiness in the marriage. She gained an accomplished and successful husband and a companion who shared her artistic interests, they reinforced each others' enthusiasm for painting. She gained a readymade family, including two teenage girls who needed the love of a good stepmother. She also gained security and a settled home, no more lodgings on Tyneside. From Robert's perspective, Isa's contribution to his well being and continued success was very considerable, her painting career though was somewhat impeded.

It was Isa who in 1895 introduced Robert to the artistic community at Staithes. The summer visit to Staithes became an important feature of their married lives and indeed of their artistic development. Every year after that their exhibits included pictures of the distinctive community at Staithes and the Yorkshire coast painted on their annual stay at Dale House, and for a time Cullercoats began to take second place to Staithes.

As well as exhibiting at Staithes they continued to exhibit in Newcastle, they both had exhibits in the Laing Art Gallery from the day it opened in 1905. Robert became a founder member of two new Newcastle Art Clubs, The Art Circle and the Pen & Palette Club, he moved his studio from Shakespeare Street to the Pen & Palette Club in 1900. In 1913 he became President of the Bewick Club, but its heyday was over, its role as the main exhibition centre had been usurped by the Laing. Robert continued exhibiting until 1922 and Isa until 1900. Robert much feted throughout his later life died in 1923 aged eighty-two. Isa continued to live in the house at Victoria Avenue until just before her own death from cancer in 1926.

It was typical of the period that Robert's work overshadowed his wife's. Women and women's work were undervalued and women's work sold at consistently lower prices than men's. This was as true of Isa Jobling as of any other woman painter. Today however Isa's paintings command prices at least equal to her husband's. Isa's marriage to Robert Jobling did constrain and even change her work. She was certainly much less prolific than her husband. In the twenty-seven years of their marriage, she exhibited only sixty paintings whereas he exhibited 135. However, it is now thought that after the marriage some of Robert's best works were painted *collaboratively* with Isa, for she had a better eye for composition and could paint figures better than he.

The quality of Isa's own works remained high but there is nothing in her later work which compares with the scale and ambition of the *Fortune Teller* or *Fisher Folk* for example. Her paintings seem smaller and are mainly of flowers and landscapes. The works she exhibited at the Royal Academy after her marriage bear this out. The subject matter is indicated in the titles - *Lone Reaper* (1897), *The Crofters Harvest* (1898), *Anna* (1900), *In the Orchard* (1904), *A Seaside Garden* (1908) *and A Country Rose* (1912).

However, Isa emerges from the shadows as a woman of strength and ability. John Millard concludes that even when her subjects were modest, her paintings frequently outstrip Robert's in technique and freshness of vision. Isa's great achievement is that having embraced fully the supportive role of a married woman in Victorian England she managed to continue to produce work of such high quality and today, art critics say she was in fact the better artist.

In recognition of the joint contribution of the Joblings to the artistic heritage of the region an exhibition was held of their work at the Laing Art Gallery in 1992. It was the first major showing of Robert's work for seventy years and the only major showing of Isa's work.

Isa Jobling's legacy is her paintings, two of which can be seen locally*, Fisher Folk* at the Laing Art Gallery, and *Haymaking* at the Shipley Art Gallery in Gateshead.

A colourised postcard of
Sister Winfred Laver.

Sister Winifred Laver BEM (1888-1980) BEM

Servant of Gateshead's Poor and Destitute for sixty years

Sister Winifred Laver, a trained nurse and a deaconess in the Methodist church, arrived in Gateshead in 1915 and served its poor and destitute for the next sixty years. She arrived a complete stranger; alone and only twenty-seven years old.

Winifred was brought up in Birkenhead, one of five children whose father, Captain Laver, was a tug boat pilot. Despite the relative affluence of her own background and against her parents' wishes she decided from an early age to dedicate herself to the service of the poor. She held posts in a children's home in Oxted, Surrey, and in Cheshire, where she contracted tuberculosis. After several months recovering, and despite the advice of both her doctor and her parents, she successfully applied for a position with the Poor Children's Holiday Association to start a mission in Vine Street Gateshead. The PCHA was a Methodist foundation with its headquarters in Percy Street, Newcastle. Using charitable donations, its objectives were to provide much-needed day trips and holidays in the country for the thousands of destitute and deprived urban children in the area, but Winifred saw her brief far more widely, she worked to bring help and support to every aspect of the lives of destitute families and to win their souls over to Christ.

Gateshead was an overwhelmingly working-class town (the population in 1917 was 120,000) and during Sister Winifred Laver's sixty year ministry it remained a place of great poverty and hardship for most of its people, even those in work. Indeed in 1934 J.B. Priestley wrote of Gateshead in his *English Journey*, that it seemed to have been, 'carefully planned by an enemy of the human race,' remarks triggered by what he had seen, slums, abject poverty, pawnbrokers' shops and penny pop-shops. Unemployment was a major problem; in 1935 over 10,000 were unemployed, in 1963, over 4,000. Housing was poor; there was chronic overcrowding and appalling sanitation, which, along with a meagre diet, meant widespread disease and dirt. In every decade there were epidemics of influenza or pneumonia, scarlet fever or diphtheria. As late as 1951, Gateshead's infant mortality rate and its incidence of tuberculosis were the third worst in the country.

It was to this town that Sister Winifred Laver came, despite her doctor's warnings. She began her missionary work in October 1916 in a freezing-cold derelict building with a leaking roof, but just a month later this phenomenal lady was running Sunday and weekday services there, attended by as many as 500. In her first month alone, she visited 291 families in their homes. At her first revival meeting in 1917, as many as forty people came forward to rededicate their lives to Christ and it was from this group that she drew her first active supporters and helpers. Only two years later the mission's own magazine reported that a choirmaster and organist had also been recruited. The Vine Street Mission Choir later became quite famous locally. Sunday School numbers were so great that they soon overflowed into larger premises at Rose Street School nearby.

Soon outreach programmes were organised, tent meetings Sister called them. On these occasions Sister Winifred and her trained evangelists would hold open-air meetings to attract members from beyond the immediate environs of Vine Street. Vine Street volunteers were soon calling at houses to make doorstep converts, sometimes travelling as far as villages in Northumberland.

From the outset Sister Winifred, a qualified nurse, set up a surgery to give basic medical help wherever she could and it was always heavily attended. The mission report book for 1924, states that 1,488 attended her surgery that year. In 1923 there had been 1,787 surgery cases. One rather gruesome account in the report book tells of a starving child who presented with a nasty boil on his foot. Sister Winifred applied a bread poultice to the boil only to be told that on leaving the surgery the boy had removed the poultice and eaten the bread!

The importance of Sister Winifred's social work amongst the destitute and starving cannot be overstated. She was soon organising breakfasts for the Sunday worshippers, which gave rise to a steep increase in church attendance. At Christmas she organised meals for the needy and provided presents for children who would otherwise have received nothing. She organised annual trips on the train to South Shields, Cullercoats or Tynemouth for children who had never seen the sea. Visits were also made to a variety of places, Stocksfield and Keswick for example. On one occasion, as many as 1,200 children were taken on a trip to Tynemouth, each with a little rubber PCHA stamp on their arm lest they should get lost. On these outings the food provided for the children was a vital part of their treat.

The 1924 Report book show that 573 homes were visited and relief given in the form of 160 grocery parcels, milk, boots, bread, meat pies, eggs, bottles of Bovril, 6 cwts. of coal, clothing, dispensary letters and loans paid for. Relief at this level went on for decades. Sister Winifred also organised thrift clubs and a benevolent fund to help people pay for the funerals of family members. For 4d per week, members were entitled to a payment of £4 for an adult burial and £1.10s per child's funeral. At the end of each year any remaining money was paid out to members of the scheme. She also provided the destitute with vouchers to buy shoes and medicines, she would then go to the shop or dispensary and pay for them. Clearly Sister Winifred Laver's fund-raising and organisational skills were amazing. The Vine Street mission ran a variety of youth groups and Fellowship groups, these included Boys' Brigades, Girl Guides and Scouts. As part of her evangelising work, would-be missionaries were encouraged to undertake practical training at the Vine Street Mission, and in the years 1918 to 1929, thirty-one missionary students received practical training at the Vineyard before going on to serve either abroad or in England.

In 1937 the Vine Street mission became autonomous, with its own Board of Trustees. Sister Winifred had come to Gateshead under the auspices of the PCHA and she had worked in their building rent free. But when in 1933 the owners informed her that not only did they require rent but insisted that the building be used for purposes other than the mission, Sister Winifred quickly decided this was not acceptable. The Vine Street building could not accommodate all of the activities generated by the mission as it was, and the rental charge was too much to pay. She gathered around her some of the great and good of Gateshead and they raised enough money to buy the premises from the PCHA. During the 1940s the mission also bought the old Redheugh Pit office buildings and used them for youth activities. In 1977 the old mission building was replaced by the new Evangelical Church on Derwentwater Road opened by Sister Winifred herself. A plaque in the doorway bears her name and commemorates the event. That church and its congregation continue Sister's work to this day.

It was the practice of Gateshead Council to appoint a 'Town Missioner,' in recognition of work done for the poor, and it is little wonder that sometime in the 1930s this honour was conferred on Sister Winifred. For this she received a small remuneration. Winifred considered this enough to live on and from that date she took no salary at all from the mission. The mission reports show that whatever money was collected was spent on the needy, sometimes leaving too little to pay the mission's own gas bill.

Sister Winifred died in 1980 at the age of ninety-two, and is buried in Saltwell cemetery. Until the end of her days Winifred Laver was adamant that to serve the poor of Gateshead as she did was her great privilege.

In 1978, in recognition of her amazing work Gateshead made Winifred Laver an Honorary Freeman of the Borough. She was only the second woman ever to be so honoured. She also received the British Empire Medal. A Blue Plaque was placed on the Gateshead Evangelical Church, Derwentwater Road in 2013, it reads 'Sister Winifred Laver BEM (1888-1980) Established the Vine Street Mission in 1915. She dedicated most of her life to helping the poor of Gateshead. Made an Honorary Freeman of the Borough in 1978.' In July 2014 a Local Heroes plaque was placed on Gateshead Quayside, underneath the Tyne Bridge to honour this remarkable and selfless woman.

Gateshead in
the early 1900s.

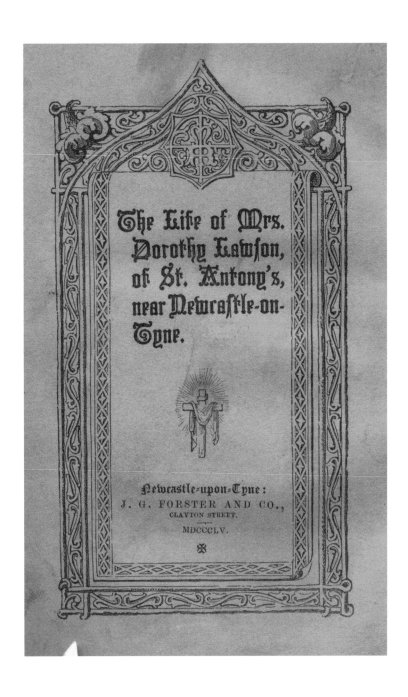

The Life of Mrs.
Dorothy Lawson,
of St. Antony's,
near Newcastle-on-
Tyne.

Newcastle-upon-Tyne:
J. G. FORSTER AND CO.,
CLAYTON STREET.

MDCCCLV.

Frontispiece of *The Life of Mrs Dorothy Lawson* by Father Robert Palmes.

Dorothy Lawson (1580-1632)

Recusant and Priest harbourer

Dorothy Lawson's bravery and dogged devotion to Catholicism in the face of grave danger were as remarkable in the seventeenth century as they are now. Her life span coincided with the savage Penal Laws of Queen Elizabeth I, designed to stamp out Roman Catholicism and Catholic priests forever. Ruinous fines and imprisonment were imposed on those who refused to give up *the ancient faith*. To harbour a priest, to be a priest or indeed for a priest to exercise his ministry, were all actions punishable by death. These penal laws remained in place until repealed in 1685 by King James II, himself a Catholic.

Dorothy was the daughter of Sir Henry Constable of Burton Constable, Yorkshire, and Margaret Dormer of Buckinghamshire. She was raised a committed catholic and at seventeen married Roger Lawson, the eldest son of Sir Ralph Lawson of Brough, in Yorkshire. It was a happy marriage and the couple had fourteen children before Roger's untimely death in 1613 or 1614. Both Dorothy's mother and Roger's mother were recusants, who had spent time in prison for their faith, but at the time of her marriage the Lawson family had all conformed to Anglicanism. None the less Dorothy was determined from the outset to remain Catholic herself, despite being fully aware that three priests had been hanged, drawn and quartered in Newcastle between 1593 and 1594. Immediately after her marriage, she arranged for regular visits from Father Richard Holtby, a Jesuit priest.

The family lived in Heaton Hall in Northumberland from 1605. After her husband's death the Hall was sold and Dorothy had a house built at St Anthony's in Newcastle, overlooking the Tyne. By then all her family were Catholic, including her in-laws and even Roger had converted on his deathbed. In fact by the time of her death she had converted the entire neighbourhood bordering Heaton and St Anthony's. The new house at St Anthony's, built to meet her domestic and religious needs, included a chapel and accommodation for Jesuit priests (perhaps also a priest's hole). Harbouring priests meant not just being able to conceal them but also hiding all their liturgical vestments and sacred vessels and disguising the fact that Masses were being held there regularly. Her biographer, Father Palmes, explains that she even placed the name 'Jesus', in large letters on the riverfront at the bottom of her new garden for the comfort of seamen and that, *'sea-fairing men of other nations might know it to be a catholick house and fly thither, as truly they did in swarmes for their spirituall refection.'*

The dangers Dorothy Lawson faced are well illustrated by the fate of some of these priests, her chaplains. On the death of her first resident priest, Father Henry Morse replaced him, but within the year he was detected and imprisoned. Father Robinson his successor was also detected within the year and imprisoned. Father W. Palmes, Dorothy's biographer, replaced him and avoided detection, serving in Newcastle, housed and supported by Dorothy, until after her death.

As well as her activities as a recusant Dorothy Lawson was widely known and loved for her good works among the poor, including visiting the sick and imprisoned, feeding the hungry, clothing the poor, assisting women in childbirth, baptising premature babies, providing a *'two penny purse'* for widows, and running catechism classes for children. These charitable activities also doubtless enabled her to make Catholic converts.

Yet despite all her missionary activity in support of Roman Catholicism, her house was never searched, she is not listed as a recusant, and she was never imprisoned or fined. The reasons are partly her connections and partly national politics. She was very well connected, affluent and could be protected. Her husband was the grandson of a former Mayor and Sheriff of Newcastle. Most local officials had recusant kin themselves or were part of the close-knit circle of Northumberland gentry. (The total population of Newcastle was only 10,000 at the time, the average number of supporters at a Newcastle football match today is 50,000.) She also had powerful relatives who might have intervened on her behalf; her uncle was Baron Dormer and her brother had a peerage. We can now see, with our historical perspective, that these laws were applied with varying degrees of intensity depending on political circumstances. The Spanish

Armada in 1588, and the 1605 Catholic-inspired Gunpowder Plot to kill the King, for example, intensified their application for several years, whereas King James I, once Catholic laymen had taken the Oath of allegiance, gradually proved lenient towards them and as far as priests were concerned, preferred to exile rather than butcher them. But none of this belittles Dorothy Lawson's bravery, between 1600 and 1632 she took life-threatening risks, she followed her conscience and she got away with it.

Her children were also brought up as Catholic and three of her daughters embraced the religious life, Dorothy as a canoness at Louvain and Margaret and Mary as Benedictine nuns at Ghent. Others married into Catholic families and later several generations of Lawsons were indicted for recusancy and became priests or nuns. Dorothy herself provided future generations with an exemplary model of piety and missionary zeal.

Dorothy Lawson died of consumption in 1632, and her funeral was quite remarkable. Her biographer writes that she was buried in All Saints Church in Newcastle the day after her death and states and that not only did the civic authorities do nothing to prevent it, they were actually part of it.

As Father Palmes S.J. recounts in his biography of Dorothy,

> ... 'Her body was conveyed in the evening to Newcastle in her own boat, accompanied by at least twenty other boats and barges and above twice as many horse... The magistrates and aldermen, with the whole glory of the town ... attended at the landing place to wait upon the coffin, ...and carried it but to the Church door,. they delivered it to the Catholicks, who with a priest laid it with Catholick ceremonies in the grave'.

Despite this today there are no public memorials to Dorothy Lawson whose great bravery was deemed treasonous.

SUFFRAGETTE

SUPPRESSED

A young Connie Lewcock cycling around Durham to sell *The Suffragette* newspaper.

Constance Mary Lewcock (1894-1980)

Suffragette and Tyneside Politician

The 'Wikipedia' entry for Connie Lewcock describes her as 'Suffragette, arsonist and socialist'. The alarming-sounding label 'arsonist' would surprise some of those present-day Tynesiders who remember her as an elderly, diminutive, twinkly-eyed, kind and effective local Councillor in the 1960s and 1970s. However Connie would not have disowned the description, and in her later years never sought to deny her involvement, as a nineteen year old, in the suffragettes' campaign in 1913 of disruption and of damage to property to draw attention to their cause.

Born Constance Mary Ellis in Lincolnshire in 1894 she grew up, and attended school in Horncastle. She was an only child, brought up in a loving, secure environment although, sadly, her father died when she was four years old. During her teenage years Connie's mother remarried, Connie's stepfather being a local Methodist Minister. Connie did well at school and after matriculation, wanting to be independent and gain employment, looked for work as an uncertificated teacher. This brought her to County Durham for the simple reason that teachers in that county were better paid than elsewhere!

Connie had been inspired by the 'Votes for Women' campaign whilst still a schoolgirl and had joined the Women's Social and Political Union (WSPU). Even as a school girl she had managed, in 1911, to save up money in order to travel to London and take part in a suffragette procession and demonstration in Hyde Park. Her first steps as a teacher in Durham coincided with her becoming further involved and by 1912 -1913 she was one of the most active and enthusiastic members of the WSPU's North Eastern section. By this time too, following on from the imprisonment, hunger strikes and force-feeding of many of the Suffragette leaders, the campaign had turned to violent protest as well as one of organised demonstrations.

The campaign of violence was however aimed at property not people, and designed to create publicity through alarm without human casualties. Only one person died during the course of suffragette protests and that was one of the Movement's own, Emily Wilding Davison.

Most of Connie's suffragette activity concentrated on speaking up at meetings and taking part in demonstrating against anti-suffrage government ministers whenever they visited the North East. However she did conspire to destroy by fire the small wooden railway station at Esh Winning in County Durham. This episode was apparently carefully planned in order to get herself identified as the prime suspect (to protect her miner friend who had actually carried out the attack) while having an unchallengeable alibi which would mean that she would escape being charged. Her friend who lit the fire left one of Connie's handkerchiefs, with an embroidered letter 'C', together with some hairgrips, at the scene of the crime. However since Connie was at a meeting at Cornsay colliery several miles away at the time of the attack and several unimpeachable witnesses testified to that fact the police, although highly suspicious of her, were unable to implicate her in the crime. Nonetheless her employers, unconvinced of her innocence, told her that she must either give up her suffragette work or forfeit her job as a teacher. She promptly resigned her teaching post.

Connie described the Esh station incident as 'a very small fire and soon dealt with but the commotion and alarm were gratifyingly great'.

It was also mooted that as part of the campaign Connie should with bellite blow up a pier in Durham cathedral but this was a step too far for her and she doubted her ability to handle explosives. In a much later interview for BBC Television in 1978 she said that she was glad, given the precious nature of the building, that such an attack had not taken place.

Connie's unpublished autobiography describes this time of her life vividly and she talks of the bonds of solidarity and friendship which united the suffragettes as can be seen in the following account of their processions and demonstrations:

'Oh those processions! They make the demos of today look like a very casual crowd. We walked in step, mentally striding into the New World to which the vote was the key. We did not chatter as we walked. At regular intervals we carried pennons or flowers in their colours. And now and again, from the crowds who lined the pavements, curious, scoffing, laughing or sympathetic, a woman would step forward and fall into line. They were a superb thing to watch and it was sublime to be part of them.'

Connie also approved of the discipline and obedience which Emmeline and Christabel Pankhurst required of their followers, feeling that this was vital to achieving success.

Her militant suffragette career was itself however brought to a sudden close with the outbreak of the First World War and the suspension of the campaign. From then on Connie's political activity was channelled into the Independent Labour Party and subsequently into the Labour Party itself.

Ironically at the start of the First World War Durham Education Authority begged Connie to return to teaching, given staff shortages, and she then took up work in a school in Brandon Village.

In 1915, on May Day in the pit village of Chopwell, 'a centre of Trade Union and Socialist Activity', Connie first encountered Will Lewcock. There was an instant attraction. Will was a miner, who had been financed by the Miners' Union to study at Ruskin College Oxford, and like Connie he was active in the ILP. He was also a registered conscientious objector - a stance which Connie fully supported

- although as a miner he was initially exempt from call-up. Their courtship lasted throughout most of the war and they were eventually able to get married in the summer of 1918, by which time Will (who as a single miner was no longer exempt from call-up) had been assigned to work, as a conscientious objector, in food production in the Middlesborough area.

Before that, in 1916, as a result of her political activity Connie had been offered, and had accepted, work as a Trade Union organiser. Some of the training for this took place in London where Connie had accommodation arranged for her by Margaret Bondfield. She was then posted to Middlesborough and had responsibility for recruiting women to join the National Federation of Women Workers. While there she also successfully negotiated an important equal pay settlement for women workers at a local paint factory. During her time at Middlesborough because of her anti-war stance Connie was accused, in court proceedings, of making 'seditious speeches likely to prejudice recruiting'. She was defended by the solicitor for the Independent Labour Party but was fined as the result of fabricated statements by 'witnesses'. The ILP paid Connie's fine - although against her wishes - and Connie records in her autobiography that many years later one of the 'witnesses' apologised to her for his part in framing her unfairly.

After their marriage Will gained employment as a Labour Party Agent in Stroud and afterwards he would hold various senior organisational posts for Labour. Connie became his active and supportive partner fully committed to the success of his work and undertaking a variety of tasks - whether as typist, secretary or assistant organiser. In the course of a long and successful marriage the couple were to have three children - Sheila, Peter and Cynthia.

From Stroud they moved to Newport where again Will was a Labour Party Agent and Connie, as a young mother, served for a time as a Labour Councillor. Then in 1931 Will was appointed Regional Organiser for the North East in York a move summarised by Connie in the words 'Geordies always want to get back home, and this was at least, a good step nearer'. They lived in York until 1942 when Will became Regional Organiser for Durham, Northumberland and Cumbria - a post based in Newcastle.

The rise of Hitler during the 1930s led Connie and Will to abandon their earlier pacifism feeling that Nazism must be resisted by military as well as other means. With the outbreak of war and fears of German invasion Connie and Will decided - because they knew they were on the SS List of those known to be socialists and anti-fascists - to apply for their youngest child twelve year old Cynthia to be included in the evacuation scheme to Canada. This was a painful decision, made after much heart searching. During the war - and with Will's new employment on Tyneside - he and Connie decided to live on a smallholding in Pelton, County Durham, which Connie would run, growing food and thereby helping the war effort. Connie from her childhood had loved the countryside. Now her love and considerable knowledge of plants and flowers would be supplemented by more practical agricultural activities!

When the war ended, and with Cynthia happily restored to the family, Connie and Will moved to Newcastle where they lived for the rest of their lives. Will retired in 1956 but sadly died only four years later in 1960.

Connie was elected to Newcastle City Council as a Labour member for the Benwell ward which she represented from 1960 to 1971. She served as Chair of the Council's Housing Management Committee. Former Newcastle City Council Leader Jeremy Beecham (now Lord Beecham) remembers her fondly and worked with her when he was first elected a Councillor - also for Benwell - in 1966. He describes her as a 'wonderful colleague' and as someone who 'was very committed to the provision of decent social housing, not least in a ward with some dreadful conditions'. Even today some fifty years later Connie's daughter Cynthia meets people who pay tribute to her mother as a wonderful woman, determined to help those in need.

Connie was awarded the OBE in 1966. In 1978 she came to Westminster Hall in the House of Commons to celebrate, along with leading politicians of the day, the 50th anniversary of the date when all women over twenty-one were given the right to vote. Also around that time she attended a service to commemorate the life of Emily Wilding Davison in St. Mary's Church in Morpeth, where Emily is buried. True to her radical past and to the memory of her suffragette comrades many people remember her at that service expostulating with indignation at the description, from the pulpit, of Emily as a reckless woman endangering the lives of men and horses!

After retiring as a Councillor, Connie continued to be active politically into her eighties and played a key role in the Tyneside Fabian Society, enjoying both their meetings and conferences, as well as the outings they organised to the Northumberland countryside and the Scottish Borders, areas which she loved and appreciated to the full.

Connie's name lives on through the Connie Lewcock Care Home for the Elderly and Resource Centre (offering a community rehabilitation service) in the West End of Newcastle on West Denton Road. She is remembered not only for her bravery and commitment to the suffragette cause but also for her record of service to the people of Newcastle and particularly those in the Benwell area to whom she was so obviously devoted. On 10th May 2018 Connie Lewcock's family received an honour on her behalf from the Lord Mayor of Newcastle, Councillor Linda Wright and from the Deputy Mayor of Gateshead, Councillor Jill Green. Connie is commemorated too with her own plaque on the 'Local Heroes Walk of Fame' which runs along the Newcastle and Gateshead Quayside.

Charlotte Augusta Leopoldine Marsh (1887-1961)

Militant Suffragette, suffered imprisonment and force-feeding

The women's suffrage movement became a national movement in Victorian times. Supporters either joined the moderate National Union of Women's Suffrage Societies, led by Millicent Fawcett, or the militant Women's Social and Political Union, known as the suffragettes and led by Emmeline Pankhurst. The suffragettes were prepared to break the law and suffer the consequences in order to achieve the vote for women. Whatever we may think of their militancy, their efforts were heroic and their dedication and personal bravery outstanding.

More than 1,300 suffragettes suffered imprisonment for the Cause. Many of them also endured the horrors of hard labour and the brutal and dangerous procedure known as force feeding. One of them was Charlotte Marsh from Newcastle.

Charlotte was the third daughter of Arthur Hardwick Marsh A.R.W.S. (1842-1909), a successful artist. He painted in oil and water colour as well as designing stained glass for the glass works of John George Sowerby in Gateshead. Charlotte, or Charlie as she preferred to be known, was born in Alnmouth, though the family later moved to Cullercoats and by the turn of the century were living in Newcastle. She was educated in Newcastle and then in Wrexham and spent a year studying in Bordeaux. She was one of the first women to be trained as a Sanitary Inspector. The 1875 Public Health Act, in trying to combat the filthy living conditions in urban areas, required every

Charlotte Marsh in Hyde Park, 1910. She was Grand Marshal for this Women's Sunday procession.

public health authority to have a Medical Officer and a Sanitary Inspector to ensure that laws on food, housing, water and hygiene were observed. Charlotte was so appalled by the insight her training gave her into the filthy living conditions endured by poor families that she decided instead to work to give women a voice in public affairs and joined the militant Women's Social and Political Union in 1907. She was twenty years old, and destined to be one of the foremost militant suffragettes.

Charlotte suffered her first term of imprisonment in June 1908, when she was arrested for obstructing the police following a W.S.P.U. demonstration in Parliament Square. She, along with others including Lena Lambert from Newcastle, were found guilty and imprisoned in Holloway for one month.

The following year she became the WSPU organiser for Yorkshire. Her role was to raise vital funds to keep the Suffrage Movement in the public eye and put pressure on local politicians. In 1910 she became WSPU organiser in Oxford, she then moved on to Portsmouth and in 1913 she became WSPU organiser in Nottingham. As well as working as a full time paid organiser, Charlotte continued to undertake militant acts.

Her second imprisonment occurred in 1909 for her part in a roof-top protest that included hurling tiles at Prime Minister Asquith's car outside Bingley Town Hall, Birmingham, where he was addressing a meeting. The police attempted to move the two women, Charlotte and Mary Leigh, by turning a hosepipe on them and pelting them with stones, but failed to get them down. Three policemen then scrambled up a ladder and dragged them down. Still in only their stocking feet, soaking wet and bleeding from their wounds they were marched through the streets to the police station. At the police station bail was refused and the two women spent the night in the cells in their drenched clothing. Charlotte was given a three-month sentence with hard labour at Winson Green Gaol. There was a great outcry at the severity of the sentence, but when Charlotte, along with Mary Leigh and Laura Ainsworth, went on hunger strike things became much worse. For the first time the authorities decided to resort to the horrible expedient of feeding them through a tube forcibly passed into the stomach. This barbaric procedure was used until the Cat and Mouse Act of 1913.

Laura Ashworth described it on her release in 1909;

'...a tube about two feet long was produced. My mouth was prized open with what felt like a steel instrument and then I felt them feeling for the proper passage. All this time I was held down by four or five wardresses. I felt a choking sensation, and what I judged to be a cork gag was placed between my teeth to keep my mouth open. I experienced great sickness, especially while the tube was being withdrawn'.

What made matters even worse for Charlotte was that her father was dying and she desperately wanted to go to him. She was due for release on 7th December but the authorities detained her until 9th December. Despite having been force fed 139 times and in a seriously emaciated condition, she travelled straight to Newcastle to her father's bedside. Sadly he was already unconscious and died several days later without knowing she was there.

Charlotte was imprisoned for the last time in 1912, for smashing nine plate glass windows in The Strand. Because she had previous convictions she received a six-month sentence, served in Aylesbury prison. Once again, she staged a hunger strike and endured force feeding.

Because Charlotte Marsh was a beautiful golden-haired young woman, tall and elegant, she was often used as standard bearer for WSPU processions. In 1908 she carried the colours in the procession to celebrate the release of Christabel and Emmeline Pankhurst from Holloway, and in June 1913 she led the funeral procession of Emily Wilding Davison carrying a large wooden cross.

With the outbreak of the Great War the WSPU announced a 'truce' with the Government, but Charlotte continued her commitment to the suffrage cause as honorary secretary of the Independent WSPU. (The organisation ceased to exist when, in 1918, the Representation of the People Act gave about 8.4 million women the vote and allowed the election of women to Parliament.) Ironically Charlotte worked during the war as a motor mechanic and chauffeuse to Lloyd George. He was fully aware of her background but wanted to employ a woman as he was campaigning for women to join the work force to replace the men fighting the war. Charlotte took the view that any contribution to the war effort would increase the likelihood of women winning the vote.

After the war, Charlotte returned to feminist politics as an officer on the Women's International League for Peace and Freedom. Following the granting of the full franchise in 1928, she devoted her time to social welfare work, and from 1934 until her retirement she worked in the Public Assistance Department of London County Council. She continued throughout her retirement to support the Suffragette Fellowship, of which she was Vice-President. Charlotte never married and died at her home, 31 Copse Hill Wimbledon in 1961.

Charlotte 'Charlie' Marsh, lived her campaigning life according to the suffragette mantra, 'Deeds not Words'. Her only legacy is the record of her bravery and her part in gaining political enfranchisement for the many.

Top) Force-feeding a suffragette. A team of wardresses pin the woman down while a doctor pushes a long rubber tube through the nostril and down into throat, allowing liquid food to enter the stomach.
Above) Suffragettes march down Northumberland Street, 1906.

National Portrait Gallery

Harriet Martineau, by Richard Evans.

Harriet Martineau (1802-1876)

Britain's First Woman Sociologist

One of the most remarkable women in nineteenth century Britain was Harriet Martineau and she has an interesting connection with the North East as for six significant years of her life - from 1840-45 - she was a resident of Tynemouth. It was in that town that she recovered her health, and was then able to continue her work and her special contribution to life in Victorian Britain.

Harriet Martineau is notable because she was one of the very few women who succeeded in the early nineteenth century to earn her own living on equal terms with men and she was also one of the very few to be recognised and respected for her ideas, for her intellect and for her contribution to hitherto exclusively masculine domains such as economics, political philosophy and social science. She is often described as Britain's first woman sociologist.

She was brought up in Norwich in a Unitarian family of Huguenot descent, in comfortable circumstances. However, when the family textile manufacturing business failed, she was forced to fall back on her own resources. Along with her brother James, she had been well educated and, in company with him, she took up writing on subjects of interest to her. Her first successful publication *Illustrations of political economy* (1832) was a work on economics that achieved wide renown in popularising the work of the economist Adam Smith. Astonishingly, when comparing monthly sales it regularly outsold the works of

Charles Dickens by a considerable margin! Harriet and James also wrote about the Poor Law reforms that were being put forward by the Whig Party in Parliament. Still in her thirties she established a considerable national reputation and a wide public following, then embarked on a tour of the United States. She successfully lectured there but also courted controversy because of her firm support for the abolitionist cause, a cause she continued to publicise on her return to Britain in her work *Society in America* (1837) and other writings.

Harriet's success and fame had brought her to the attention of Princess Victoria, who was apparently one of her keen readers. So much so that Harriet was invited by Victoria, to attend her coronation in 1838.

Harriet also enjoyed the company of a number of the most interesting people and intellectuals of the time, including John Stuart Mill, George Eliot, Elizabeth Barrrett Browning, Thomas and Jane Carlyle. She was a close friend of the Darwin family, including Charles Darwin, whose theories of evolution she was to support. There were rumours of a romance between her and Erasmus Darwin, Charles' brother, and although no engagement ever materialised Harriet remained close to Erasmus and the Darwin family throughout her life.

Harriet became keenly interested in the ideas of the French philosopher Auguste Comte and through her writings - and her translations of his work into English - his ideas on sociology became much more widely known in the English-speaking world. In part, too, through Comte's influence, her religious views were to move away from Unitarianism towards secularism and atheism. While much of her work is non-fiction she also wrote fiction with her novel *Deerbrook*, published in 1838, being particularly successful.

In the late 1830s, Harriet's health deteriorated due to a uterine tumour. Her sister Elizabeth was married to the celebrated Newcastle doctor, Thomas Michael Greenhow, and Harriet turned to him and Elizabeth for support. She moved to the North East in the autumn of 1839 to be under their care and took up residence in Front Street, Tynemouth where she lived from 1840 to 1845.

For a large part of her time she was confined to her bed, but continued writing, publishing three books during her Tynemouth stay. The first of these was her novel *The Hour and the Man*, based on life of the freed slave Toussaint L'Ouverture, who became President of Haiti - a novel that was the favourite of Harriet's great friend, Florence Nightingale. Then followed a collection of short stories for children – *The Playfellow*. However, her Tynemouth sojourn is most closely associated with her work *From the Sick Room* (1844). This work arose out of the limits to her freedom at this time of ill health, which had led her to reflect on the different circumstances that constrained people's lives and in particular the way that women's lives were frequently circumscribed. It was praised greatly by Wordsworth among others.

In Tynemouth Martineau developed and consolidated some of her thoughts on women and society and the need for women's lives to be an integral part of the study of society. Her recognition as Britain's first woman sociologist stems in part from this period. When in the United States she had decried the very limited educational opportunities for women there, a theme that she expanded on during her Tynemouth years, although she saw women's education as needing to involve both the domestic and the academic sides of life. She also wanted, alongside politics and religion, attention to be given to such issues as class and race relations, views that were innovative at the time.

In Tynemouth Harriet was offered but declined, for the second time, a pension from the civil list in recognition of her literary work. She refused because she never wanted to be seen to compromise her intellectual independence, yet given her straitened circumstances at the time it must have been a tempting proposition.

Despite the confined nature of her life in Tynemouth, Harriet Martineau had affection for the town and her surroundings. In particular, she loved to watch the activities of the river and glimpse the lives of local people. With the aid of her telescope she became fascinated by the clear night skies exclaiming; 'What a heaven! What an expanse of stars above, appearing more steadfast the more the Northern Lights dart and quiver!'

In 1845 her health had improved to the extent of allowing her to reaffirm her independence. She attributed the cure to mesmerism, although this unconventional treatment was not wholly approved of - or believed - by her doctor brother-in-law Greenhow.

Harriet loved the Lake District and from Tynemouth moved to Ambleside, where she lived until her death in 1876. It is the Lake District that, perhaps more than any other part of the country, now claims her as its own. However, her Tynemouth residency, both because of the writings she produced there and her family connections, remains an important part of her life' story. Her years in Tynemouth are marked by a blue plaque on the house in Front Street where she lived and the house is now, appropriately, the 'Martineau Guest House'.

Sister Kate Maxey with a Royal Army Medical Corps orderly.

Sister Kate Maxey (1876-1969)

Distinguished Nurse of World War One

Kate Maxey, who was born in Spennymoor, County Durham, became one of the most highly decorated nurses of the First World War.

Kate was the daughter of John Maxey, a shopkeeper with premises on the High Street in Spennymoor. There were three other children, Martha, John and Amelia. By the time Kate was fifteen years old, she had left her home and was living in Leeds with her Aunt and Uncle, Dr and Mrs McKane, she wanted to be a nurse and had obtained a position in Leeds Infirmary. She trained and worked there, qualifying in 1903. (In those days nurses rarely started nurse training before the age of twenty-three). In 1912, she joined the local Territorial Force Nursing Service, (TFNS) based at the 2nd Army North General Hospital, Leeds General Infirmary. The TFNS was founded in 1908 to care for the members of the volunteer Territorial Army. In peace time TFNS Nurses worked full time at their normal nursing duties and made only a part-time voluntary commitment. When war broke out, however, they were all promptly drafted to serve on the Western Front.

Before the outbreak of war in 1914, there was already a national shortage of qualified nurses, less than 1,200 for a population of 37 million - and these and many more were soon needed in France.

The war made unprecedented and unforeseen demands on all medical staff. During the course of the First World War over 9 million soldiers died and casualty numbers were even greater. Soldiers' wounds were of a severity and scale never before encountered. High velocity bullets tore tissue and splintered limbs, mud and manure infected wounds and gangrene was rife. This war saw the invention of the tank and the introduction of chemical warfare in the form of chlorine and then mustard gas. Bayonets and hand grenades caused serious injury. Trench fever, trench foot and infectious diseases also felled many soldiers due to conditions in the trenches. All of this predated antibiotics. Medical staff worked under constant pressure from the huge numbers of wounded soldiers, the horrific nature of their injuries, as well as the makeshift nature of many of the medical facilities and the constant danger of enemy fire and bombing raids.

As soon as war broke out hospitals and casualty stations were established and doctors and nurses in their hundreds were drafted to serve them. Kate Maxey was sent to Rouen in October 1914 and from then until March 1918, she gave unstinting and distinguished service at several hospitals on the Western Front. She worked at Wimereux General Hospital No 14, and at No 1 General Hospital at Etretat. While at Etretat, Kate became friends with Edith Elizabeth Appleton, the diarist, whose accounts of her work in the hospitals of Northern France have provided vital first-hand information about the experiences of soldiers and nurses during these dark years. In 1916 Kate Maxey was promoted to sister and served at Abbeville hospital. In September 1917, Kate was appointed Sister in Charge of the 58th Casualty Clearing Station at Lillers. It was here, in March 1918 that she was severely wounded. During a bombing raid an ammunition train exploded near the casualty station. She sustained multiple bomb wounds to the forehead, the neck, the right leg and the right foot, as well as a broken arm and spinal injury. The officer commanding the Casualty Station wrote, 'Miss Maxey's tact, zeal for work and influence for good are of the highest order ... When lying wounded she still directed the nurses, orderlies and stretcher bearers, and refused aid until others were seen to first .... one of the finest Nursing Sisters I have ever met'. These injuries put an end to her four years' service overseas, however she did recover and after convalescing with her sister in Spennymoor, she spent the remainder of the war nursing in Leeds, before being demobilised in June 1919.

Sister Kate Maxey was awarded the Royal Red Cross Medal 1st Class in 1914, for distinguished service in the field and gallantry during the bombing raid. The Military Medal was awarded to her in 1918 for bravery under fire. In 1920, Kate was one of the very first recipients of the Florence Nightingale Medal awarded by the International Red Cross Committee 'for nursing services from 1914 to 1918, especially at No. 58 Casualty Clearing Station'.

After the war Kate worked in Heathroyde Nursing Home in Halifax, until her retirement in 1931. She returned to Spennymoor and died in Bishop Auckland, County Durham, aged ninety-three.

Elizabeth Montagu (1718–1800)

Queen of the Blue Stockings, Literary Patron, Author and Coal Magnate

For fifty years in the eighteenth century Elizabeth Montagu was known as, 'the leading light of literary London'. What is less well known is her connection with the North East of England; she was a frequent visitor to the family manor house, Denton Hall, on the West Road in Newcastle and became owner of the Montagu Colliery.

Born in York, Elizabeth was the first daughter and fifth child of Mathew Robinson and his wife Sarah Morris. Both parents were wealthy and well connected. Elizabeth and her sister Sarah were avid students and precocious children and their grandfather, Conyers Middleton, a prominent Cambridge don, tutored both girls in Latin, French and Italian as well as English literature and history.

Elizabeth's connection with the North East began when, in 1742 aged twenty-four, she married Edward Montagu, the incredibly wealthy fifty year old grandson of the first Earl of Sandwich, the owner of coal mines in Northumberland as well as estates in Yorkshire and Berkshire. They had one son, born in 1744, who died in infancy. There were no further pregnancies and although Elizabeth and her husband remained good friends, they led separate lives until his health began to fail in the 1760s and she attended him with care until his death in 1775.

As a young woman, Elizabeth's ambition was to become a social and literary luminary and, supported by her considerable fortune, by the 1760s she had established herself as the most lavish of society hostesses who insisted on intellectual and literary conversations as opposed to card parties. Quadrille and cribbage were forbidden, as was strong drink. Her salon was held in her London homes, in Hill Street, Mayfair and then in the sumptuous Montagu House, Portman Square (built in 1782 with money from husband's estate). The success of these mixed gatherings attracted many famous people, Fanny Burney, the novelist and diarist, famous by age of twenty-six, Hannah More, the great moralist and do-gooder of the period, Elizabeth Carter who had published her

first book of poems by the age of twenty in 1738. London's leading men also graced her salon, Samuel Johnson, Sir Joshua Reynolds, Edmund Burke, David Garrick and Horace Walpole were regulars. From these salons developed the literary circle known as the Bluestockings. The epithet was meant to indicate the informality of the evenings and arose from the casual worsted blue stockings worn by Sir Benjamin Stillingfleet when he attended the soirees. Black silk stockings were more normal attire. By the 1770s, an introduction to Hill Street was the favoured route for struggling writers to gain patronage from the wealthy hostess.

Elizabeth Montagu's claims to be a literary figure herself depend on her scholarly, *Essay on the Writings and Genius of Shakespeare*. In it she defends Shakespeare against the attacks made by Voltaire. The piece was translated into French and Italian and ran to four editions. Although published anonymously, as was the custom for women authors, her name did appear on the fourth edition. Elizabeth was also a copious letter writer and a few of her thousands of epistles were published during her life. Today all her letters have been published and like those of Hugh Walpole and Mary Delaney, are among the most important surviving collections of the eighteenth century, indeed Elizabeth's letters are now considered her major contribution to literature.

Edward Montagu's death in 1775 was preceded by a long illness and so, from 1758 until 1789, Elizabeth frequently visited the Montagu collieries and Denton estates, taking responsibility for their management, which she relished. Unusually, Edward left his entire estate to his wife, and not to a male heir. She received an annual income of £7,000 and lived for twenty-five years as a wealthy widow in the most advantageous position possible for a woman in the eighteenth century, financially and legally free from the control of any other person.

Fully up to the challenge, Elizabeth set about growing her assets and developed the East Denton Colliery into a major enterprise of twenty-nine pits. At the time of her death her income from coal alone was worth £10,000 a year. She also began a building programme; at Sandleford she enlarged her mansion and engaged another great northerner, Capability Brown, to landscape the grounds, and she commissioned the building of Montagu House at 22 Portman Square in London, where in 1791 she entertained the King and Queen and 700 guests. She was thought a generous employer and provided picnics and treats for her tenants and colliers, including an annual feast for chimney boys. Having said that, she wrote, 'Our pitmen are afraid of being turned off and that fear keeps an order and regularity among them that is very uncommon'. She was generous in the provision of annuities for some of her literary friends, Hannah More, Anna Laetitia Barbauld and James Beattie, among them. There is plenty of evidence that when in Newcastle she also enjoyed an energetic social life. When Elizabeth died aged eighty she left her estate to her nephew Mathew Montagu.

Elizabeth Montagu was widely admired for her knowledge, her brilliance in conversation, her ready wit and sound judgement. Dr Johnson said of her, *'She diffuses more knowledge than any woman I know or indeed almost any man'.* Whilst she was also lampooned for her extravagance, there is no doubt that she helped refine contemporary London. Having established the blue-stocking assemblies she rescued fashionable London from the tyranny of whist and strong drink. She also helped create a new view of women as intellectually able and equally receptive to ideas and argument as men. She contributed to the prominence of women writers in the eighteenth century. Her management of her estates was witness to her business acumen, she demonstrated that women could look after their own property very well. It is important to note that the patronage, the parties and all the wealth she enjoyed, were generated by the coal fields of Newcastle and Northumberland.

Top) On the House of Commons terrace. Above) Mo Mowlam speaking at the Labour Party Conference 1997 at Brighton.

Right Hon Marjorie ('Mo') Mowlam (1949-2005)

Cabinet Minister and Northern Ireland Peace Negotiator

'Our one and only Mo' (Tony Blair)

To write about someone whom I knew well as a personal friend and treat her as a historical figure is a challenge because it is difficult to be objective and detached. However it is also a pleasure to pay tribute to someone who has left her friends and the wider public so many vivid and warm memories.

Although she was born in London and went to school in Coventry, Mo Mowlam has a strong claim to a place in this book as throughout her political career, for which she is primarily remembered, she was Member of Parliament for Redcar. Furthermore Mo was a graduate of Durham University where she studied from 1968 to 1971 and later worked from 1979 to 1983 as a Lecturer in Politics at Newcastle University.

Mo was the second of three children having an older sister and a younger brother. Her early childhood was happy and carefree but became more difficult sometime after the family move to Coventry when the problems of her father, Frank, with alcohol became more apparent. This affected the family greatly but also seems to have made Mo determined to study and get on with her life, academically and socially, as best she could. Despite her family difficulties she became Head Girl at school, did well at 'A' levels and gained a place at Durham University. She took an early interest in politics by first becoming interested in disarmament issues and supporting CND. She also gained local publicity by campaigning, with a couple of school friends, to clean up the Lady Godiva statue in Coventry City centre which had become covered in verdigris. A picture of her in the local newspaper was accompanied by a story lauding the schoolgirls for putting the local Council to shame by their efforts!

At University in Durham, Mo combined intelligence with a free spirit and a zest for living. Always irreverent and occasionally outrageous she was great fun to be with. Despite her informality and light-heartedness she was, nonetheless, a serious academic. After taking her degree at Durham she successfully completed a doctorate at the University of Iowa and lectured at Florida State University. She came back to the UK in 1979 to the North East when she was appointed, in 1979, Lecturer in Politics at Newcastle University.

While in Newcastle she became involved in the Labour Party both locally and more widely. She was active in her local constituency but also helped Neil Kinnock's campaign to become Party Leader in the summer of 1983.

She had expressed interest in standing for Parliament and had hoped to be selected for her local Tyneside seat but it looked in the run-up to the 1987 election that her chances of becoming a candidate were fading. However just before the general election was called the sitting MP for Redcar announced his retirement and from a shortlist of four Mo was selected.

She made an immediate impact in the House of Commons being a young, attractive, articulate, blonde woman at a time when only six per cent of MPs were female. In her maiden speech she paid particular tribute to Ellen Wilkinson who had represented part of the Redcar seat some sixty-three years previously.

Mo was one of the first members of the 1987 intake to be appointed to the Labour Front bench when in 1988 she was made shadow Minister for Northern Ireland. This proved to be a significant appointment given Mo's subsequent responsibilities. Mo then had a number of other shadow roles including being spokesperson for the City, her energetic efforts to promote a positive relationship between the Labour Opposition and the City of London being dubbed by the press 'The Prawn Cocktail Offensive!' During her time as City spokesperson Mo also first met Jon Norton whom she was to marry in 1995.

Mo was elected to the Shadow Cabinet from 1992 onwards, and to Labour's National Executive Committee in 1995. By 1996 she was therefore a key Parliamentary player and certain to be a member of Cabinet under a future Labour government. However 1996 was also to be a crucial time in her life for another reason for at this time, after feeling unwell for a few months she was diagnosed with a brain tumour and had to undergo a course of treatment including radiotherapy and steroids. Apart from her husband, stepdaughter, personal assistant and Tony Blair, as her Party Leader, the nature of her illness was at first not disclosed to anyone and to all intents and purposes her workload and commitments continued virtually unabated.

Her appearance changed considerably and was remarked upon - although her weight gain was attributed to the fact that she had given up smoking. A particularly unkind press description of her 'an only slightly effeminate Geordie trucker', together with the announcement of an imminent general election, spurred Mo to make a public declaration about her state of health which she did with characteristic courage and flair. She also declared that she was rather fond of Geordie truckers and became a pin-up girl in many a North Eastern lorry cab as a result!

When the Labour Government was formed in 1997, Mo Mowlam was appointed to be Secretary of State for Northern Ireland. She was admirably suited to this post having had shadow responsibilities for Northern Ireland at different times in the preceding years and having acquired, too, a deep knowledge of the territory and its people, meaning that unlike many new Ministers she did not have to embark on a steep learning curve but was able to set to work purposefully straightaway. With her open, outgoing and caring persona she was an instant - even a sensational - hit. She mixed with crowds in walk-abouts and memorably engaged directly with those she met in a thoroughly approachable way. Her already considerable public popularity soared.

She also handled some volatile situations successfully and courageously. She helped to restore the IRA ceasefire and was key in ensuring that Sinn Fein joined in the multiparty talks to try to get agreement on Northern Ireland's way forward. She was also prepared to engage in high risk strategies such as visiting the Maze prison in order to try to persuade personally some of the most dangerous convicted loyalist prisoners to commit themselves to the peace process. In these and other ways she contributed much to the Good Friday Peace Agreement of 1998 which established the principles of power-sharing and agreement concerning the political and constitutional status of Northern Ireland.

In such a situation - and even for such a popular politician as Mo - it is impossible to please everyone and her informal, sometimes outrageous, style seemed to work better with the nationalist parties and with the public than with some of the official Ulster Unionist politicians, who preferred to deal with Tony Blair direct. In any case, given how high a government priority the Northern Ireland situation was, it was always likely that the Prime Minister's own team as well as that of the Northern Ireland Secretary, would be heavily involved and as long as both were working towards the same goal this was highly desirable.

Mo also worked very well with the US President Bill Clinton and his wife Hillary who referred to her as our 'delightful new friend'. The US Special Envoy to Northern Ireland, George Mitchell, described Mo as follows: 'She is blunt and outspoken and swears a lot. She is also intelligent, decisive, daring and unpretentious. The combination is irresistible.'

Despite the stressful and constantly challenging nature of the work Mo enjoyed life in Northern Ireland and hosted memorable weekends at Hillsborough Castle for an eclectic collection of friends from politics, the arts and other spheres. In addition to the traditional garden parties held by the Secretary of State she organised a special one for Northern Ireland children to which two children from every school were invited. She was keen to open up the gardens of Hillsborough Castle to the public and spared no effort in seeking to re-establish and 'normalise' Belfast to become a city that people elsewhere in the UK and Ireland would want to visit and enjoy.

In October 1999 Mo's term of office in Northern Ireland came to an end when, in a Government reshuffle, she was appointed Cabinet Office Minister. This role was much less congenial to her and she described it as 'Minister for the *Today* Programme' meaning that it was a job for defending government policy without making much input into it. She was however in charge of the Government's Anti-Drugs policy as well as playing a coordinating role in government generally. Her friends know too that at the time she had ongoing health concerns and the aftermath of the brain tumour left effects which were depressing at times for her such as the fact that her once beautiful hair failed to grow back fully.

Mo stood down from Parliament at the election of 2001. She published her memoir *Momentum: the Struggle for Peace, Politics and the People* in 2002. Her personality and public profile made her attractive to broadcasters. She was the subject of a *This is Your Life* programme in 2003, she starred in *Room 101* and took part in a programme about 'the Greatest Briton' advocating support for the eventual winner of the public's vote, Winston Churchill. She worked as Agony Aunt for *Zoo*, and set up a charity 'Mo-Mo helps' to support disabled children and drug rehabilitation projects.

Politically she remained engaged, and became a critical friend of New Labour in opposing Tony Blair's decision to go to war in Iraq, and signalling her concerns that there was a drift away from some of the policies she held dear. She continued to be close to many colleagues she had worked with throughout her political life.

Mo Mowlam died in 2005 from complications relating to her brain tumour. Her ashes were scattered at Hillsborough Castle and in Redcar. At an unforgettable Memorial event in the Theatre Royal, Drury Lane, on 20th

November that year her husband Jon read a poem he had written about her and tributes were paid by Betty Boothroyd and others. To conclude the event we all sang the appropriately irreverent Monty Python song *Always look on the bright side of Life*. Very sadly her beloved husband Jon only survived her by four years, dying at the age of fifty-three in 2009.

It is now twenty years on since the Good Friday Agreement was finalised and there have been celebrations to mark this anniversary. Mo's unique contribution to the Agreement should not, despite the fact that she is no longer alive, be forgotten. As her step-daughter Henrietta Norton has written in a tribute published in the *Guardian* newspaper not only did Mo play a key role in the negotiations leading to the agreement she, by her positive approach and her ability to bring people (especially women) from the different communities together, created a climate in which those crucial steps towards peace and reconciliation could be made.

A memorial mosaic to Mo was installed in Redcar in 2009, representing her life and interests and, very appropriately, a children's park created in the Stormont Estate in Northern Ireland was named after her. There is a portrait of her in Parliament and she is also remembered in many buildings she officially opened such as the Joseph Swan school in Gateshead.

Royal College of Obstetricians and Gynaecologists

Ruth Nicholson.

Dr Ruth Nicholson (1884-1963)

First World War Surgeon and Medical Pioneer

Many of the first women allowed to qualify as British doctors played an important part in the First World War, despite the hostility of the British Government towards them. There were only 600 registered women doctors in 1914, and although little has been written about their war work, the heroic life of Doctor Ruth Nicholson, born and bred on Tyneside, provides us with an excellent case study.

Ruth was born in 1884 in 32 Kenilworth Road, Elswick, Newcastle upon Tyne, the eldest of the six the children of the Rev Canon Ralph Nicholson and Margaret A. Nicholson. Ruth attended Newcastle High School and made the decision to study medicine at an early age. She registered at Newcastle College of Medicine, Durham University in 1904, the only woman in her year, and graduated as a doctor in 1909. After working in a dispensary in Newcastle, Ruth went to Edinburgh, to the Bruntsfield Hospital, and became assistant to Dr Elsie Inglis, the renowned Scottish Doctor and suffragist. She then travelled to Palestine and worked in the mission field to gain more surgical experience.

With the outbreak of War, Ruth returned home to help in the war effort and joined a medical voluntary unit preparing to go to France. She was ready to board a train at Victoria when she was turned away by the doctor in charge because he refused to have a woman on his team! For an ardent feminist like Ruth, this was quite a blow! However, this rebuff worked in Ruth's favour as she joined the Women's Scottish Hospitals in Edinburgh and became a vital member of the Staff of Royaumont Hospital, (Hopital Auxiliare 301). She worked there continuously from its inception, in November 1914, until the Hospital's closure in March 1919. As principal surgeon and second in command to Dr Frances Ivens, she helped to found this small medical unit and transform it into 'the' crack hospital of the First World War.

At the declaration of war, the National Union of Women's Suffrage Societies resolved to suspend its campaign for the vote and devote its energy to the war effort. Members wanted to establish mobile hospital units as close to the Front as possible and thus treat the wounded as quickly as possible. This idea was the brainchild of Dr Elsie Inglis, secretary of the Scottish Federation of Women's Suffrage Societies, affiliated to the NUWSS. This was the beginning of the Scottish Women's Hospitals for Foreign Service (SWH). As the title suggests, these hospitals were to be run and staffed exclusively by women recruited from all parts of the UK. They were entirely funded by British, American and Canadian donations, money raised by the NUWSS through a network of fundraisers. The NUWSS also drafted press releases and influenced organisational details, and came up with the idea of encouraging donors to sponsor individual hospital beds.

Only days after war was declared, the SWH committee had raised £5,000, enough to provide two, one-hundred bed hospital units. They offered them to the War Office and then to the British Red Cross. But remarkably both turned them down! Indeed when Dr Elsie Inglis went to the War Office in person to make this offer, she was told they were not needed, and 'to go home and sit still woman'! Undeterred, the women then offered their medical units to Britain's allies. The Belgians and the French were first to accept, and, with astonishing speed, the first Scottish Women's Hospital was opened in Calais in November 1914. By December 1914, the second was opened in the ruins of the Cistercian Abbey of Royaumont, France.

These were not the first all-women units in France. Doctors such as Louisa Garrett Anderson and Flora Murray (Women's Hospital Corps) and Florence Stoney (Women's Imperial Service League) had set up similar units in Paris and Boulogne, but the largest organisation was the SWH. In all seventeen SWH units were established in Serbia, Corsica, Greece and Romania and 1,500 women served in them. Royaumont was the largest British voluntary hospital, the second nearest to the front line and the only one to operate continuously from January 1915 to March 1919.

The thirteenth century Abbey at Royaumont was an empty medieval relic, thirty miles north of Paris, in a beautiful woodland setting but damp and dirty, with little heating, no electricity and no water supply when the SWH agreed to turn it into Hopital Auxiliaire 301, a hospital of 100 beds fully equipped for the reception of surgical cases and answerable to the French Red Cross.

SWH sent a team of thirty-two, led by Dr Frances Ivens and Dr. Ruth Nicholson to achieve this transformation. By sheer guts and good humour, and with funds provided by the NUWSS, the hospital at Royaumont was deemed operational in January 1915.

The wounded arrived by train at Creil, and were then driven the twelve miles to the hospital. The size and role of the hospital evolved to meet the different needs of the war and uniquely, in quieter times it treated civilian patients. At the height of the war it was the largest of the voluntary hospitals in France, with 600 beds. In the spring of 1917 Royamount was extended when they established a new clearing station, nearer to the front line at Villers-Cotterets, about fifty miles north east of Paris, in a deserted wooden evacuation centre. It provided a further 231 beds and a staff of over thirty.

Surgical work was intense throughout the war. By 1918 there were between twelve and sixteen (women) doctors working between the two hospitals, including between nine and eleven surgeons led by Ruth Nicholson. Hospital records show that in a period of twenty-four hours on April 7-8 1918, as many as eighty operations were carried out. In June 1918 there were 1,240 patients admitted and 892 operations performed. The context was the grim reality of an operating theatre in wartime, the stench, the pain, the blood and the amputations. At the busiest times the doctors would get only three hours rest in twenty-four hours.

The nature and scale of the injuries inflicted on soldiers in France during the First World War were unlike anything previously experienced. Multiple wounds were inflicted from high explosive shells and rapid machine gun fire. The high velocity of the bullets meant that soil and clothing, as well as metallic fragments, were driven deep into the tissues where they formed a focus for infection. In France the well-manured soil was heavily contaminated, and harboured the bacteria responsible for the deadly gas gangrene.

'The most terrible of all the horrors which come under the care of the surgeon in war is undoubtedly gas gangrene. Dramatic in the suddenness of its onset, the rapidity of its advance, and the repulsiveness of its too frequently fatal outcome, it has reaped a cruel harvest of our young and vigorous manhood." Dr Agnes Savill, Royaumont 1916.

In 1914, before the discovery of antibiotics, there was no knowledge of how to detect, prevent or cure gas gangrene. It was the most urgent and major medical problem, and it was in this field that the women at Royaumont made their major contribution to the advance of medical science. They worked with Professor Weinberg of the Pasteur Institute in Paris, in trying to find an anti-gas gangrene serum. Professor Weinberg wrote that he chose to work with Royaumont because he had 'seen hundreds of military hospitals, but none, the organisation and direction of which won his admiration so completely.'

At Royaumont they adopted interdisciplinary procedures to deal with gas gangrene. They used X- ray and bacteriology for diagnosis, then surgery to remove infected tissue, and finally they applied Professor Weinberg's serum. This allowed them to fight infection and avoid unnecessary amputations. The total number of patients treated between Royaumont and Villers-Cotterets hospitals was 10,861. Of these 8,752 were soldiers and among the soldiers the death rate was only 1.82%. These results were widely acknowledged to be spectacular.

Royaumont Hospital was also renowned for its fully equipped X-ray car, and the use of the innovative open-air wound treatment. The location and beauty of the place also aided recovery. The fact that it was as happy a place as possible also helped the men's morale and their recovery. Ruth Nicholson played a full role in creating this legendary ambience and in the seasonal entertainments laid on for the soldiers her role as the Big Bad Wolf in the hospital pantomime of 1916 was second to none. She acted the part of a dancing dervish, as one of her concert turns, and her scarf dances it seems were unforgettable! She is referred to time and again as a dedicated, skilled, kind and jolly person, admired by all.

For her remarkable services to the wounded during the First World War, Ruth, received the coveted French military award, the Croix de Guerre in 1918 alongside Dr Ivens and thirty of her Scottish Women's Hospitals colleagues. She also received the Medal of Gratitude, and the Medal of Honour from the Ministry of War for Epidemics.

After the War Dr Ruth chose to specialise in obstetrics and gynaecology and became Clinical Lecturer and Gynaecological Surgeon at the University of Liverpool. She was a Foundation Member of Royal College of Obstetricians and Gynaecologists in 1929, and in 1933 was made a Fellow of RCOG. She was a founder member of the Women's Visiting Gynaecological Club and became the first woman President of the North of England Society of Obstetrics and Gynaecology.

Ruth retired to South Devon and continued to attend the Royaumont

Hospital reunions until the end of her life. When she became ill she was nursed by one of the former Royaumont Hospital sisters, such was the love and loyalty she inspired. Ruth Nicholson died in 1963 in Exeter aged seventy-nine.

There is no blue plaque nor any other permanent public recognition of Doctor Ruth Nicholson's life though there are many references to her in Eileen Crofton's book, *Angels of Mercy. A Women's Hospital on the Western Front 1914-18.* Durham Record Office and the Medical Women's Federation have documents relating to her. A memorial to the redoubtable founder of the Scottish Women's Hospitals, Dr Elsie Muriel Ingels has recently been unveiled in Edinburgh Public Library.

IWM

Dr Frances Ivens inspecting a French patient at Royaumont.
Painting by Norah Neilson Gray.

The first woman to study Mechanical Engineering at the University of Cambridge, Rachel Parsons.

Rachel Parsons (1885-1956)

Engineer, Founding President of the Women's Engineering Society and Campaigner for Women's Employment

Rachel Parsons lived and worked on Tyneside until she set up her own home in London at the age of thirty-seven. Despite being born into a privileged and brilliant engineering family, she worked throughout her life for equal opportunities for women of all classes, particularly in employment and especially in engineering.

Rachel was the daughter of the great engineer, inventor of the turbine engine, Sir Charles Parsons. Her mother, Katharine, was an engineer and campaigner for women's rights in the North East. Rachel's grandfather, the Third Earl of Rosse, was President of the Royal Society 1848-1854, and Rachel's grandmother, Mary Rosse, was an astronomer and pioneer photographer. There can be no doubt that a love of science and engineering were in Rachel's blood.

The family, Rachel and her brother, Algernon George, nicknamed Tommy, lived in Elvaston Hall, Ryton, then at Holeyn Hall, in Wylam, Northumberland. After Tommy's death in 1918 the family moved to Kirkwhelpington in Northumberland, to a huge 10,000-acre estate called *Ray Demesne,* which Rachel retained until 1950.

Throughout the First World War, Parsons Engineering Companies in Newcastle, at Heaton and Wallsend, played a vital role in winning the war, supplying turbine engines for warships and the steam turbines to generate vast quantities of urban electricity, as well as searchlights and other optical munitions.

From the outset Rachel showed a great interest in science and its application. Her father encouraged her in this and they spent hours together making model engine-driven machines. As a child, Rachel was aboard the *Turbinia* for its speed trials. Powered by the Parsons steam turbine, *Turbinia* proved to be faster than all the other sea-going vessels of the day and from that time the Parsons steam turbine was used to power all British warships, dreadnoughts, and all ocean-going super-vessels such as the *Lusitania*, the *Mauretania* and the *Titanic*.

Rachel attended Newcastle High School and, in 1900, was sent to Roedean School for Girls, founded to prepare girls for the newly opened women's colleges at Cambridge, Girton and Newnham. In 1910 Rachel went to Newnham College and became one of the first women ever to read Mechanical Science at Cambridge. She took Part One of the Tripos and passed the qualifying examination for Mechanical Sciences in 1912 and thus became a qualified engineer.

But there it was supposed to end, even for Rachel! The gender stereotyping of the day meant there was a huge prejudice against the employment of women as engineers. Trade Unions opposed them, fearing that they would take jobs from the men, employers felt it was not worthwhile training women whom they felt should stay at home, and society in general felt that engineering was just not women's work.

However, with the outbreak of the First World War in August 1914, and the departure of two million men to fight, the employment situation changed dramatically. Suddenly it became essential to employ women in huge numbers in heavy industry and engineering. This posed huge problems.

For Parsons Marine Steam Turbine Company at Heaton, help was at hand in the person of Rachel. In the absence of her brother Tommy, Sir Charles invited Rachel to replace him as an 'alternative' Director on the Board of the Heaton works. Her main responsibilities were the recruitment and training of women to replace men. Rachel jumped at the chance. In 1915 Lloyd George created the Ministry of Munitions and Rachel Parsons joined their training department, recruiting and instructing thousands of women to perform a multitude of mechanical and engineering tasks in the factories on Tyneside. The jobs included installing electrical wiring for battleships, assembling aircraft parts, working hydraulic presses and all aspects of shell production.

Rachel also became a leading member of the National Union of Women Workers, founded in 1895 and campaigned for 'Equal pay for Equal work'.

During the Great War, in the face of a national emergency, over one million women were recruited into engineering jobs. Gender stereotyping had to be set aside! Women proved that they could do this work and do it well and the whole country was full of praise.

However, after the War, things changed dramatically for women, sometimes for the better. In 1918, some 8.5 million women over thirty years of age were enfranchised, women over twenty-one were allowed to stand for Parliament and the removal of the Sex Disqualification Act allowed women entry into some professions, for example medicine and law. But the end of the war also spelt economic disaster for thousands of women. All the special war work was at an end, industry was contracting and such jobs as there were had to be kept for the returning soldiers. The Trade Unions reverted to type and were adamant in their refusal to admit women to engineering, and, worst of all, in 1919 the Restoration of Pre-War Practices Act swung into force. All women in engineering jobs at the end of the war had to give them up unless they worked for firms that had employed women before the war. It was assumed that women would all go quietly back to their homes and everything would be as before but that was impossible, not least because the war had increased the number of single women, so that by 1918 one in three women had no income unless they worked.

Rachel Parsons herself was a victim of the attempted restoration of the pre-war order. Tommy's death in action in 1918 devastated the family, and her father, whom she had always idolised, refused to allow her to convert her alternative directorship at Parsons Marine Steam Company into a full directorship to replace Tommy. Rachel could not accept her father's decision and, perhaps unwisely, she resigned immediately. This event was traumatic for Rachel and she bitterly resented her father's decision for the rest of her life.

In response to all of this, and convinced by the engineering talent and skills women had shown throughout the war, Rachel began her twenty year campaign to open up engineering as a career for women. The main vehicle for this campaign was the Women's Engineering Union, which she founded in 1919 in response to the Restoration of Pre-war Practices Act.

She and her mother, Lady Parsons, together with Caroline Haslett, founded the W.E.U. to encourage the retention of women engineers after the war and to actively promote engineering as a rewarding career for women. Rachel became its first President in 1919. She argued that just as Florence Nightingale and Elizabeth Blackwell had struggled hard and successfully for the right to do work of their own choosing, so it should be with engineering. Initially the difficulties they faced were enormous; the weight of Government policy, the wrath of the Trade Unions and a hostile press. However, gradually, and with hard work and some outstanding role models, the closed doors of the skilled trade unions did eventually yield as did the professional engineering institutions.

Examples of protégées of the Women's Engineering Society include Claudia Parsons (not related to Rachel), who became a pioneering mechanical engineer, one of the very first women in England to graduate in engineering and the first woman to circumnavigate the globe by car. Dorothee Pullinger became the first woman to be admitted to the Institute of Automobile Engineers in 1924 and Dorothy Buchanan became the first woman to be admitted to the Institute of Civil Engineers in 1929.

In 1920, Rachel helped create an all-female engineering firm, Atlanta Ltd., based in Loughborough with her mother as Chairman and a principal shareholder. The firm produced hand-scraped surface plates 'guaranteed accurate to ten thousandths of an inch', oil burners, inventors' models and accurate machining. It ran successfully for eight years, during which time Rachel was part of the workforce.

Many of the learned societies and professional institutions had a history of being exclusively male. The Royal Society, for instance, refused entry to the brilliant Hertha Ayrton until 1922, when they had to accept her in the wake of the Sex Discrimination Removal Act. The Linnean Society issued a posthumous apology to Beatrix Potter for the sexism it displayed in handling her research in 1897. So whenever an opportunity came to breach barriers and gain membership, Rachel Parsons took it in the interests of equality and because it gave her a new opportunity to make her voice heard. She became a member of the Royal Institution of Great Britain in 1918, a lifelong member of the Institute of International Affairs in 1921, and was admitted to the Institute of Naval Architects in 1922.

In 1922, Rachel, a wealthy unmarried woman, left the family home and set up her own household in Portman Square, London and there she began to host social events for the great and good of the day; today we might call this networking. That same year, always seeking a broader canvas, Rachel was elected to London County Council and served on the Electricity and Highways Committee. In 1923 she stood for Parliament as the Conservative candidate for the constituency of Ince in Lancashire, but was defeated. Merely to stand for Parliament was trail-blazing as Lady Astor had become the first women MP only four years earlier. As late as 1940, Rachel put her name forward for adoption as Conservative parliamentary candidate for Newcastle North, but was unsuccessful.

Throughout a twenty year period after the Great War, Rachel Parsons and her colleagues successfully devoted a great deal of energy to women's employment rights and the campaign to open up engineering to women.

Rachel's great legacy is the Women's Engineering Society, still in existence today it continues to support women who are now positively encouraged to work in all the engineering disciplines. By the end of the 1920s all the great institutions of the engineering profession had admitted women to their membership. When, in 1939, the Amalgamated Engineering Union decided it would admit women, 100,000 female engineers joined almost immediately.

Long after Rachel retired, the momentum she and others created continued to gather pace. Women today enjoy access to all forms of engineering and can delight in the fact that Jane Wernick, CBE. F.R.Eng. played a major role in the design and construction of the iconic London Eye. Today, one in eight of the engineering workforce is female and the President of the Royal Academy of Engineering is Dame Ann Dowling.

Sadly Rachel Parsons' own life ended tragically. In her later years she had developed a passion for horse racing, and was living in Newmarket when on 2nd July 1956 she was found murdered in her own stables, bludgeoned to death. Dennis James Pratt, an ex-employee, was later convicted of her manslaughter.

Women workers in a turbine factory.

Mabel Phillipson, Gaiety Girl turned MP
for Berwick upon Tweed.

Mabel Philipson
(1887-1951)

Gaiety Girl and the North East's First Woman MP

Who was the North East's first woman Member of Parliament? The chances are that most people who might be asked that question would probably in their answer hesitate between the Labour MPs Margaret Bondfield and Ellen Wilkinson. The surprising but correct response would be Mabel Philipson, the Conservative MP for Berwick upon Tweed between 1923 and 1929. Mrs. Philipson was only the third woman ever to take up her seat in Parliament and her life story was both unusual and colourful.

Like the first two women MPs to sit in the Commons, Nancy Astor (in 1919) and Margaret Wintringham (in 1921) Mabel Philipson 'inherited' her seat from her husband Hilton Philipson, whose election had been declared invalid because of financial overspending by his agent (of which Hilton Philipson had been unaware). However her background was different to that of both Lady Astor and Mrs Wintringham and she can be described as the first working class woman to take a seat in Parliament, having been brought up in Peckham in south London in humble circumstances. She was also the first British-born Conservative woman to be elected to the House of Commons and the first to successfully introduce a Private Member's Bill and get it into law.

Before becoming involved in politics she was a nationally known - and glamorous - musical comedy actress and 'Gaiety Girl'. Despite these achievements, and the intriguing nature of her rise to prominence, she is little remembered today and there is no full length biography about her.

Mabel's childhood in a working class household in 1890s south London was made more difficult by the death of her mother when she was only eleven years old and when she found herself sharing responsibility for the upbringing of her younger brother and sister. After leaving school she looked for ways to earn money and, being attracted to the theatre, gained employment in the Box Office of the Shakespeare Theatre in Clapham, South London. By all accounts a very attractive and outgoing young woman, she was offered parts in local productions and took the chance to shine and impress when she was asked to stand in for a principal pantomime character who was taken ill.

Her first big part on the national stage was as 'Fifi' in *The Merry Widow* and she became well known as one of the famous 'Gaiety Girls'. At the turn of the twentieth century in Edwardian London these girls were seen as fashion icons and as talented entertainers, and (in contrast to earlier views of women in the theatre) as symbols of ideal womanhood. Many Gaiety Girls became famous and respected actresses - Cicely Courtneidge, Ellaline Terris and Gladys Cooper, for example.

Mabel met her first husband during her time at London's Daly Theatre. He was Stanley Rhodes, a wealthy Northern cotton manufacturer, and a nephew of Cecil Rhodes (founder of Rhodesia). Stanley was an early motorcar enthusiast and tragically, when he was only twenty-two and less than a year into his married life with Mabel, he was killed in a crash at Brooklands. Mabel, who was a passenger with him, was badly injured. She recovered although she lost the sight of one eye.

While being left comfortably off, Mabel must have found such an early and sudden widowhood both sad and lonely as after a while she decided to return to the stage. From musical comedy she moved into straight acting in such well-known venues as the Haymarket Theatre and Wyndham's. At Wyndham's she was hugely successful in the 1916 Production of *London Pride* and it was there that she got to know one of her admirers, Captain Hilton Philipson, a North Easterner from Tynemouth and an aspiring National Liberal politician. They married in 1917.

Hilton Philipson was selected as the National Liberal Candidate for Berwick on Tweed to fight the 1922 election. The contest attracted publicity since it was a contest between two 'Liberals' - Walter Runciman, former Cabinet Minister was the official Liberal Candidate and Hilton Philipson was the 'National Liberal' candidate supported by Prime Minister, David Lloyd George.

Philipson attracted Conservative as well as National Liberal support and won with a 4,500 majority.

His electoral triumph proved very short lived. When, after his agent was found guilty of corrupt electoral practices, he was disqualified from standing for Parliament for seven years (although personally exonerated from wrong-doing) it was mooted by some of his supporters and voters that his wife could 'keep the seat warm for him' a suggestion which, given Mabel's great local - and national - popularity, was taken up widely. Mabel herself, although willing to accept nomination, stated firmly that if she stood it would be as a Conservative candidate rather than fighting under the 'National Liberal' party label of her husband, already showing that she could be political in her own right. She showed herself to be an effective campaigner, engaging with agricultural and countryside issues, as befitted her large, rural constituency. At the bye-election, held in 1923, she won by an impressive 6,000 votes.

The arrival of a bye-election victor in the House of Commons is always a noteworthy occasion but in this instance, with the election of a glamorous and well-known actress and one of only three women out of a total of over 600 men, it was an event that attracted huge media and Parliamentary attention. Five months later, Mabel made her maiden speech in a debate on unemployment. She did not shy away from controversy, criticising the opposition for its socialist credo, but also spoke as a woman, and referred to the effects of unemployment on women and children, conscious that as a woman MP in an overwhelmingly masculine House of Commons she had a duty to speak up for that half of the population who had just become (partly) enfranchised.

Mabel was re-elected in the general elections of 1923 and 1924 and served as Member of Parliament for Berwick until the election of 1929 when she stood down.

During her time in Parliament she focused frequently on constituency interests including fishing, farming, the hardships faced by agricultural workers and the quality of rural housing and transport. However she also raised more general issues such as the difficulty ex-servicemen of the First World War experienced in finding suitable housing and employment opportunities, and spoke on issues of vital concern to women and children including on bills relating to the guardianship of children and on seeking to remove the stigma of illegitimacy upon children born out of wedlock.

She also successfully introduced a bill to regulate and license nursing homes - the Nursing Homes (Registration) Bill - which was passed in 1929 and is still on the statute book today. As Pamela Brookes wrote in *Women at Westminster* 'this was a much needed measure to exercise control over private establishments, many of which left a great deal to be desired'. Furthermore she handled a bill on behalf of its sponsor who was unable to take it through its stages in the Commons to make the registration of theatre managers compulsory. Given her theatrical career this was an appropriate measure for her to promote and it duly became law.

In 1928 she was offered a junior Ministerial position at the Department of Health, an offer that she declined, probably for family reasons and because she had already decided against trying for a further Parliamentary term. She was the mother of three young children and on one occasion she was forced to defend herself in the Commons when she was criticised for having missed some Committee meetings by referring to the fact that one of her children had been ill. It is easy to imagine that in a House with only a handful of women the demands on a working mother were not always well understood.

Despite her theatrical training, Mabel Philipson did not find it easy to address the House of Commons and found its environment somewhat alien. This did not stop her speaking when she felt she had to, but her speeches are short and she limited herself to subjects where she felt compelled to intervene. She did have a reputation of being a good advocate behind the scenes however - managing to persuade Ministers of her constituents' needs and lobbying for legislation in areas where she felt action ought to be taken.

She announced her retirement in 1928, citing family responsibilities. The needs of her children, in particular of her disabled son Peter, and difficulties within her marriage seemed to be the key reasons.

After retirement from Parliament she returned to the stage for occasional guest appearances. Indeed she had never entirely deserted the theatre even in her Parliamentary days, appearing in a lead role in *The Beloved Vagabond* during a Parliamentary recess - something that aroused interest and comment, both positive and negative. Her last appearance - in London's West End - was at Wyndham's theatre in 1933.

In retirement she lived quietly with her family in Sussex, keeping in touch with friends from showbiz years and attending occasional Gaiety reunions and birthday parties. She died in 1951 aged sixty-four.

Perhaps because after her retirement from politics she was out of the limelight for a relatively long time, little has subsequently been written about her, but her touching rise from poverty and her unusual route into politics, as well as her achievements in getting elected and in passing legislation that remains on the statue book today, deserve recognition and permanence in the chronicles of women's political emancipation and participation in public life.

Dr Marion Phillips (1881-1932)

Outstanding Women's Organiser

Another woman whose links with the North East were short-lived but memorable was Dr Marion Phillips, Member of Parliament for Sunderland for two years from 1929-1931.

Her background was an unusual one. She was an Australian citizen, born into a Jewish family, her father being a lawyer in Melbourne. Marion was a clever scholar and after graduating from Melbourne University she came to the London School of Economics to study for her doctorate. While there she became involved in politics through Sidney and Beatrice Webb (co-founders of LSE and the Fabian Society). She greatly impressed the Webbs, who nominated her in 1906 to be a special investigator on the Commission set up to investigate the workings of the Poor Laws. This work also subsequently involved - as a co-investigator – Dr Ethel Williams.

Marion soon became immersed in Labour politics and quickly demonstrated organisational as well as academic ability. She became a member of the Women's Labour League and took over as its Secretary, succeeding Margaret Bondfield in 1912. In 1919 she was appointed Chief Woman Officer of the Labour Party, a post she was to hold until her death in 1932 and which she filled with skill and great distinction.

She built up Labour's Women's Organisation impressively, to the point where it comprised some quarter of a million members nationally. Women's Sections were established at constituency level and these became a key part of local Labour parties. The role of Labour women, in her eyes, was not just a campaigning role helping to elect Labour councillors and MPs but was a way of promoting the political education and advancement of all women and thereby fostering the increasing participation of women in public life.

She toured the country speaking, becoming a well-known national figure. A formidable person, she was nevertheless dubbed affectionately 'Maid Marion' by her Party. She took up many causes of interest to women, including equality in the workplace, the provision of school meals, children's clinics and play spaces. She campaigned for improved sanitation and repeatedly called for all new housing to be provided with proper bathing and washing facilities. Not surprisingly, having benefitted from higher education herself, she wanted all women to have real educational opportunities.

Besides her work for women in Britain, Marion was keen to promote the international movement of women's organisations. She helped form the International Federation of Working Women and was also prominent amongst those pressing for women to be represented at the League of Nations.

Her travels brought her to the North East on many occasions, where she had a loyal following, particularly from the Durham Labour Women's Advisory Council, one of the biggest and best-organised women's divisions in the country. It may have been this that prompted her to stand as candidate in Sunderland in the general election of 1929, as might also the support from Sidney Webb, who by that time was MP for neighbouring Seaham.

Being a candidate in Sunderland brought her face-to-face with the pressing social and economic problems of the town. Marion seems to have been very forcibly struck by the economic and social hardship she witnessed. She campaigned untiringly and in the election of 1929 came top of the poll in Sunderland's two-member constituency. In her maiden speech in Parliament, she spoke compellingly of the high levels of unemployment and dire housing conditions in Sunderland and claimed it was probably 'the most distressed town in the country', with one in four out of work. Even those in work - in the shipyards in particular - were badly paid and their wages were being reduced not increased, as she indignantly pointed out.

During her time as Sunderland's MP, she was so eager to jump up and down to seek to speak on behalf of her constituents that she earned the nickname 'the Kangaroo'! Yet, although undeniably active on behalf of Sunderland in Parliament, she still continued her work as Labour's Chief Woman's Officer and lived in London.

Along with most of her Labour colleagues she lost her seat in 1931 and sadly died from cancer at the beginning of 1932, aged only fifty, at a time when, given her experience, she would have had so much to contribute. Although her main achievement was her national work for Labour women there is no doubt that her short time in Sunderland led her to take the town and its people to heart. The people of Sunderland were equally impressed by her and her commitment to them as their Parliamentary representative.

Anna Richardson (1806-1892)

Leading Anti-Slavery Campaigner

Until recently, Anna Richardson was in danger of being forgotten even in Newcastle, the town where she spent her adult life. Happily however, the recent celebrations of the 50th Anniversary of the granting of an honorary doctorate by Newcastle University to Martin Luther King have served to bring back into the limelight the earlier efforts to promote African American equality of this remarkable Newcastle resident.

Anna Richardson, nee Aitkins, was born in Chipping Norton to Quaker parents and went to school in Ackworth, West Yorkshire. It was there that she met a fellow pupil Henry Richardson whom she would subsequently marry. Like Anna, he was a Quaker and the son of a tradesman in the grocery business.

After their marriage Henry and Anna moved to Newcastle and they lived in Summerhill Grove, off Westgate Road, together with Henry's sister Ellen. The marriage was childless which, whatever private regrets this may have caused, may help to explain why Anna's energy became focussed on a number of public good causes. She had the clear support of her husband and sister-in-law who shared her views and were associated fully with her efforts.

Anna was interested in supporting local charitable work to help the lot of Newcastle's poorest, as well as getting involved in national and international causes.

Locally she was a prison visitor, she took a keen interest in widening educational opportunities for the children of poor families in Newcastle and she promoted temperance and teetotalism, even establishing temperance refreshment rooms in the city. She also worked to help resettle refugees.

Nationally and internationally she supported peace initiatives, such as Elihu Burritt's 'League of International Brotherhood', which was set up in 1846 and which aimed at reducing conflict and war between countries and limiting the use of armaments. Burritt visited Newcastle in 1846 and it seems likely that Anna heard him - and met him - at that time. He helped found the Newcastle Peace Society, which Anna became involved in, and he actively encouraged the participation of women in the international peace movement. Anna and her husband also attended the 1849 International Peace Congress in Paris, presided over by Victor Hugo.

Anna's main international focus of attention however was undoubtedly her opposition to slavery in the United States of America and it was for this cause that she used her considerable organisational and literary skills to maximum effect. With the outlawing of both slavery and the slave trade in Britain, the continuance of slavery in the United States was a cause many British abolitionists took up with determination and Anna was no exception.

Anna was particularly keen to bring an awareness of the cruelty and injustice of slavery to children growing up in the United States as she felt that they held the key to securing an eventual abolitionist victory. She edited a journal *The Olive Leaf*, which was particularly aimed at children and young people. She also published a children's book, in 1859, entitled *Laura; the Kentucky abolitionist*. Anna and her husband had links with many well-known campaigners and writers against slavery including Harriet Beecher Stowe who stayed with the Richardson family during a visit to Britain in 1853.

Anna was one of the British leaders of the 'Free Produce Association', which was an organisation supporting a boycott of goods produced by slave labour. She sponsored a nationwide speaking tour to bring the Free Produce campaign to the notice of towns and cities throughout Britain. Locally she established the Newcastle Ladies Free Produce Association in 1846. She also edited the magazine *The Slave*, which was the magazine of the Free Produce Association from 1851-1854.

However, it is through her fundraising campaign to buy the freedom of Frederick Douglass that she is mainly remembered. Frederick Douglass had been born a slave and had been the property of different owners during his youth. The wife of one owner had - unusually - encouraged him as a child to learn and gain some education but a later owner beat him regularly for aspiring to be educated above his station. Douglass escaped slavery in 1838, managing to make his way from Maryland to Philadelphia and then to New York, helped by Quaker abolitionists. His capacity to learn and educate himself was awe-inspiring as were his powers of oratory and persuasion. Douglass's supporters financed his journey across the Atlantic in 1845. He arrived first in Ireland and then continued on to the UK. He toured the UK extensively, including Newcastle and stayed with the Richardson family in Summerhill Grove. Anna and her sister-in-law Ellen realised that the only way he could return to the United States (both to be reunited safely with his wife and be able to campaign openly against slavery) would be if he were legally free and so together they raised the £150 necessary to procure his official emancipation.

Apparently there was some unease and criticism from abolitionists that buying Frederick Douglass' freedom legitimated the idea that freedom from slavery was a monetary commodity - however Frederick Douglass himself fully appreciated and supported what Anna and Ellen were doing and recognised that their efforts were absolutely crucial to allow him to fulfil his life's work. His freedom was duly legally granted in 1846 and the following year he returned to the United States. From then on, he was a towering figure in the Abolitionist cause. His Washington DC home is now a national monument and he is one of the major heroes of African-American - and US - history.

Frederick Douglass retained huge affection for his English supporters such as Anna. In his own words it was when he met them that, for the first time in his life, he 'was treated not as a color, but as a man'. In his work *My bondage and my freedom* (1855) he pays warm tribute to Anna herself, recognising her as the leader in the campaign to purchase his freedom, and describing her as 'a very clever lady, remarkable for her devotion to every good work'.

Anna Richardson died in 1892 and is buried in Elswick cemetery. On February 26th 2018 a plaque was unveiled on her home in 5 Summerhill Grove, the plaque also records Frederick Douglass's stay at the house and recognises the achievements of his Newcastle friends in obtaining his freedom from slavery.

The freedom of Frederick Douglass - bought by the fundraising campaign of Anna Richardson.

Muriel Robb,
Wimbledon Ladies
Singles champion in
1902.

Muriel Evelyn Robb (1878-1907)

England Ladies Singles Tennis Champion

Muriel Robb was a truly outstanding tennis player who accomplished what no tennis player has achieved before or since. Her record is unique in a number of ways; she remains the only person in the North East of England to win the Ladies Singles Championship at Wimbledon. No other player has succeeded in winning all four of the championships of the United Kingdom; the English, Welsh, Scottish and Irish Championships. No other singles championship has equalled the number of games, fifty-three, of the 1902 Ladies Wimbledon final. Sadly for Muriel, she is the only winner of a singles title at Wimbledon to die so young, aged only twenty-eight.

Born in Jesmond, Muriel was the only child of William David Robb, a corn merchant, and Ellen Robb (nee Dixon). The Robbs were a wealthy Hexham family who owned Robbs department store in Hexham.

Muriel learned the rudiments of tennis on the family tennis court in Haldane Terrace, and in 1893, aged fourteen, she joined Jesmond Lawn Tennis Club, where her mother was a member. Later the family moved to Tudor Villa in Osborne Road, only a few hundred yards from the tennis club. Muriel and her mother played regularly and two years after joining, they won the Club's Doubles Trophy.

Muriel was sent to Cheltenham Ladies College from 1893 until 1897. This was the foremost girls' school of the day; the Principal was Miss Dorothea Beale, the inspirational feminist educationalist and suffragist.

In 1896, she began to enter tournaments and that same season she won the Northumberland and Durham doubles, and a year later, the singles. The Sunderland Open quickly followed and she began to win most of the tournaments she entered. She had developed as a tennis player of some talent. She was a tall, athletic girl with a particularly strong forehand and a weaker backhand. Her powerful and pioneering overarm serve and the quality of her baseline play made her a formidable opponent. It was already clear that as well as her tennis prowess she had a good 'match' temperament and the concentration and perseverance necessary to become a champion tennis player.

She first played at Wimbledon in 1899, when she reached the quarter finals. That same year she won the Welsh National Championship and the Derbyshire Championship, beating the redoubtable veteran, Blanche Hillyard.

In 1900 Muriel again reached the Wimbledon quarter finals and won her first Wimbledon title, the Ladies Doubles, with Alice Pickering. That same year she retained her Derbyshire title, beating Blanche Hillyard again, and won the Derbyshire Women's Doubles. Later in the year she travelled to Germany and reached the final of their national championship.

Remarkably, in 1901 Muriel won two national championships, the Irish Ladies' Singles Championship and the Scottish Ladies Championship, but again she lost in the quarter finals at Wimbledon.

In 1902 Muriel made a fourth, and as it happened, final attempt to win the coveted Wimbledon Championship, and this time she did it! Her opponent, Charlotte Cooper Sterry, was an Olympic Champion and four times Wimbledon Champion.

The Match itself was arguably the strangest women's final ever. The first set was taken by Mrs Sterry, 6-4. Muriel won the second set 13-11, after which rain stopped play. The next morning, instead of resuming the game at one set all, inexplicably the stewards decided the match should be restarted. Muriel went on to win a further two sets, 7-5 and 6-1. The Ladies had played fifty-three games over a gruelling two days. This remains a record for a women's singles final at Wimbledon. Their feat becomes even more remarkable when we remember Edwardian tennis dress; a floor length dress, fitted blouse, corset, tie, belt and a straw hat!

In 1903, Arthur Wallis Myers wrote in, 'Lawn tennis at Home and Abroad,'

'To Miss Muriel E Robb has fallen the distinction of wresting for the first time since 1894, the Ladies' Championship out of the possession of either Mrs Hillyard or Mrs Sterry, and that her triumph at Wimbledon was the outcome of well-nigh perfect lawn tennis, and a fitting crown to a highly successful career, there can be no question. Indeed I doubt whether any championship round has ever produced such a magnificent demonstration of vigorous play as Miss Robb gave. Her command of the ball was so striking, her forehand drives so deadly, and her overhead serves so effective, while her self-possession was so apparent, that even Mrs. Sterry, trained hand as she is, was often at a disadvantage and forced almost throughout the contest to act on the defensive.'

That same year, 1902, Muriel won the All England Women's Doubles championship with Alice Pickering and the mixed doubles championship with George Hillyard. 1902 was certainly Muriel Robb's *annus mirabilis;* she was at the peak of her powers and a very popular young star. She, and everyone else, expected her to defend her titles the following year. However it was not to be.

Little is known of events over the next few years. Her name is simply absent from any tournament records after 1902. Jesmond Tennis Club Minute Book shows that she resigned her club membership in 1903. This must have been due to ill health. On 12th February, 1907, Muriel Robb died at her home in 81 Osborne Road. She was twenty-eight years old. The death certificate says that she died of a cancer, 'Lymph adenoma, which she suffered for two years and four months, and from exhaustion and cardiac failure.'

Muriel was buried at Jesmond Old Cemetery and the press reported that 'so many flowers and wreathes were sent that two lorries were required to transport them.'

Most recently Muriel was remembered by the city of her birth when, on the 13th of June 2011, the Lord Mayor of Newcastle, unveiled a Blue Plaque on the gates of Jesmond Lawn Tennis Club to honour her.

ITV

Well-loved agony aunt and popular author, Denise Robertson.

Denise Robertson (1932-2016)

Novelist and Well-loved 'Agony Aunt'

In her endearing autobiography *Agony - don't get me started!* Denise Robertson reveals that throughout the whole of her life she never lived more than five miles from her birthplace in Sunderland.

Although totally rooted in her native North East, Denise, particularly through television, became a household name as a favourite TV agony aunt as well as enjoying a national reputation as the author of many well-loved novels and short stories.

She died in 2017 and the obituaries that paid tribute to her many achievements and to her warm and totally genuine persona also described her life as a 'roller-coaster' an accurate description in so many ways as throughout her eighty-two years she had faced so many financial and emotional crises.

Denise was the younger - by ten years - of two daughters in a close-knit family. However financial problems beset the family from just before her birth, with her father's shipping company failing through an untrustworthy business partner who had persuaded him to invest unwisely. At the moment of Denise's arrival, the family's house was under a repossession order and they subsequently moved to council accommodation in Sunderland's Grangetown. Money was tight during Denise's early years - with only occasional relief afforded by wealthier relatives.

When she was five years old the Second World War began, and although life continued to be difficult Denise's father regained a sense of purpose through his war work as an ARP officer. At the end of the war, Denise, aged eleven, won a scholarship to the independent Church High School but remained conscious that other girls were from wealthier backgrounds, a problem exacerbated by her mother's advice –'don't let them know where you live' - not wanting to own up to living in a council house. Denise started to bunk off school and eventually, after counselling, she transferred to Bede Grammar School in Sunderland where she did well at 'O' levels. Although obviously bright, with a talent for English literature in particular, she was keen to leave school and get a job and start earning, and did so against the advice of the school's Headmistress.

Her first job was as a clerk in the Fracture Clinic of Sunderland Royal Infirmary. She graduated quickly to become medical secretary and not only did administrative work but consoled and comforted patients and their families and in particular supported and sustained many children with debilitating ailments. Her experiences there were to inspire her later writings and inform her work as an Agony Aunt.

During the 1950s, Denise had a number of boyfriends - and a brief engagement - but eventually found deep happiness with an older beau, Alex Robertson, a Shetlander and a seafarer. Once married they settled near to Denise's parents in Sunderland but then, after Alex had left seafaring to become Assistant Harbour Master in Seaham, they moved to a terraced house in that mining community. The job was not well paid but meant that Alex was home-based and he and Denise could enjoy the babyhood of their young son Mark together.

During these years in Seaham, Denise became active in the local community including serving a term as a local Councillor. She also began writing, penning some articles for the Sunderland Echo and getting some short stories accepted by the BBC. She then won a BBC new writers prize for her play *The Soda Fountain*. Alex's pride in his wife's achievements were to be short-lived as he was diagnosed with lung cancer and died, leaving Denise a widow with their son Mark only eight years old. 1972 was truly an 'annus horribilis' for Denise as she mourned the loss of her husband, coming on top of the previous losses of her father, sister and mother. Within the space of a very few years and when she was still young she had become the sole family survivor and a widow.

Denise went through a very dark period of depression, becoming addicted to tranquillisers and anti-depressants, and became very withdrawn. Only Mark tied her to life and reality. Mark had school friends and was particularly close to the four children of a neighbour, a widower, Jack Tomlin, who had lost his wife to leukaemia.

Jack was a respected local builder and through their children he and Denise, became close and decided to marry. Once again however times were difficult and challenging. Denise continued to battle her need for valium and while becoming deeply attached to her stepchildren worried about whether, as a second wife, she was second best to the memory of her husband's first love. Feelings of this kind were developed into the plot of her novel *The Second Wife* published much later. At this time she continued to write short stories and also got a job as an Agony Aunt on Metro Radio. Her ability to understand the problems of listeners was enhanced, no doubt, by her own family stresses and the consequent depression that had plagued her over the previous years.

While she became stronger emotionally and recovered her resilience and inner strength, economically the 1970s was not an easy decade and building work for Jack was in short supply. Then a financial disaster befell him when, after winning a valuable order for rebuilding a local club, the building took fire during a fireman's strike and Jack's firm was put into liquidation. Denise's income from writing and radio work became essential to the family's survival but although becoming increasingly well-known, making ends meet continued to be a constant and pressing challenge.

In 1984 the miners' strike began and Denise witnessed the misery of her local community and of the striking miners, their wives and families. She was active in supporting local relief efforts while deploring the clash of, as she saw it, 'two massive egos' that of the miners' leader Arthur Scargill and the Prime Minister, Margaret Thatcher. She co-founded a trust to help the unemployed in her area, funded by the Manpower Services Commission. Her national profile was becoming established through such roles as Agony Aunt with the BBC's *Breakfast Time* and appearing on programmes such as *Any Questions*. Her writing, which had developed from short stories to novels, continued apace.

Further broadcasting and writing successes helped tackle the backlog of debts that had been accumulated and eventually she and Jack were able to find a house - and importantly a garden - to suit them. She began her most memorable period in television as Agony Aunt on ITV's *This Morning* in 1988 - a post which was to define her for the next nineteen years and cement her reputation as a national treasure. She became the face of many national and local charities being an early campaigner for tackling AIDS, promoting anti-famine and anti-poverty initiatives in Africa and working with Princess Diana on activities promoted by 'Relate'. In the North East she became the key personality associated with the 'Bubble' foundation, a nationally famous charity supporting the pioneering work with immune-deficient children, which was based at Newcastle's General Hospital.

Denise also contributed a regular column to the *Newcastle Journal* commenting on national and local issues.

Denise's lasting legacy will probably be her novels, which draw on many aspects of her own life. She is a woman's writer in the sense that her novels are virtually all told from a woman's standpoint and she excels in describing women who cope with adversity, facing sometimes similar challenges to those that Denise herself had faced and overcome. Many women, particularly North Eastern women, are devoted readers but her books appeal to both sexes and for men seeking to understand women they are arguably essential reading! Her novels have authentic local colour, whether it is the Durham pit village of Belgate which features in so many novels, or Durham City or her beloved Sunderland. The descriptions of Sunderland reveal the author's love of her home town as well as conveying to those who don't know it and who might be tempted to think of it as 'just another industrial city' as a place of antiquity, of culture and of learning in addition to its proud industrial heritage.

The 'Beloved People' trilogy was Denise's favourite amongst her novels but the prize winning *Land of Lost Content* as well as *Remember the Moment* and *The Stars Burn On* are also compelling narratives with credible characters who evoke empathy as they face eternal challenges and dilemmas. All in all she published some twenty novels.

Denise and Jack forged a successful marriage and Denise was a loving mother both to Mark and to Jack's four sons. Their house was home to a succession of dogs, mostly strays and rescue animals. The marriage lasted twenty-two years. Sadly however not long after he and Denise could enjoy life without financial worries Jack died from a stroke in 1995.

Touchingly, after being widowed twice and having overcome so many problems Denise found late and deep happiness with Bryan Thubron, a widower and someone she had known in her youth. They lived in recent years in East Boldon in a house near her favourite pub and her favourite auction room - a house with a beautiful garden created by Bryan. These later years seem to have been very happy and secure with Denise retaining her national popularity and being treasured by the people of the North East.

Denise contracted pancreatic cancer in early 2016. In February of that year she made this information public and faced this illness with her typical strength and fortitude. She died on 31st March of that year.

Denise was awarded an honorary doctorate from Sunderland University, an honorary fellowship from St. Mary's College University of Durham and, in 2006, was made MBE. She was also a Deputy Lord Lieutenant of Durham County. Denise Robertson House in Swalwell, Gateshead, where the FACT Charity, which offers cancer support services, is based was opened in her honour in December 2016.

Dame Flora McKenzie Robson (1902-1984)

Dramatic Actress of Stage and Screen

The North East has claimed the great actress Flora Robson as one of its own and has honoured her accordingly. Durham University awarded her an honorary Doctorate of Letters in 1958, in 1961 the Newcastle Playhouse at Jesmond was renamed the Flora Robson Playhouse and a street has been named after her in South Shields. However, Flora Robson came to belong to the whole nation, she was celebrated and enjoyed throughout the country and indeed internationally. A legend in her own lifetime, she was made a DBE, Dame Commander of the British Empire in 1960, Finland presented her with the Order of the Rose and she had the further honour of having two portraits in the National Portrait Gallery in London. There are no fewer than five blue plaques to commemorate her life and work, in London, in Brighton, and Welwyn Garden City.

Flora was born in South Shields in 1902, the sixth child of David and Eliza Robson. Her father was a marine surveyor. When Flora was only five years old the family moved to Palmers Green in North London and later to Welwyn Garden City. Flora was educated at Palmers Green High School and at seventeen she went to the Royal Academy of Dramatic Art

Many of Flora's Scottish forebears were engineers, none of them were actors, but from a very early age Flora enjoyed recitation and first appeared on stage in a school production when she was five years old with her rendition of Little

Archive PL / Alamy

Flora Robson in
Fire Over England
(1937).

Orphan Annie. Her father encouraged her love of theatre and believed that she had special acting talents and that she might become the next Ellen Terry.

She graduated from RADA in 1921 and although she won a bronze medal, the years immediately afterwards were not promising for Flora. She had no theatrical family connections to call upon, she had no money and she lacked the good looks required for leading ladies, added to which at 5' 10', she was very tall for a woman.

After a two-year period struggling to stay in work, she made the heart-wrenching decision to leave the stage and for the next four years worked as a Welfare Officer in the Shredded Wheat factory near the family home in Welwyn Garden City. Her only consolation was the success of the little drama group she established there for the factory workers. Her big break came when her friend Tyrone Guthrie persuaded her to come back to the theatre and join his Old Vic Company. She had the opportunity to play a series of classical roles which gained her critical and popular acclaim; they included the stepdaughter in Pirandello's *Six Characters in Search of an Author*, and Varya in T*he Cherry Orchard*. In the early 30s, her brief appearance as the doomed prostitute in James Bridies's *The Anatomist*, put her firmly on the road to success. The Observer critic wrote, 'If you are not moved by this girl's performance, then you are immovable.' Flora was set to become one of the finest dramatic actresses of her day and by 1933 Flora Robson, born in South Shields, was leading lady at the Old Vic.

From that date Flora was constantly in demand. She won the London Standard's prestigious Best Actress Award for her stage performance in Henry James' *The Aspern Papers* in 1959. She also made a name for herself as a character actress on Broadway. She was thrilled to have a theatre named after her in her native North East and came to Newcastle to play at the Flora Robson Playhouse in 1962, in T*he Corn is Green* and again in 1964 when she played Lady Bracknell in *The Importance of being Earnest*.

She became a great star of the silver screen in both England and Hollywood. She twice played Queen Elizabeth I on screen, in *Fire Over England* (1937) and *The Sea Hawk* (1940). Some of the scenes from *Fire Over England* were featured in Second World War propaganda films. In 1945 she was honoured with an Oscar nomination for her role as the protective mulatto servant of Ingrid Bergman in *Saratoga Trunk* (1945). Flora was widely praised for her versatility, and went on to embrace television as another medium for her acting. She played Miss Pross in a lavish American TV production of *A Tale of Two Cities* and appeared on British television. Although she retired from the West End stage when she was sixty-seven, she continued to accept roles in film and television well into her seventies.

In the course of her long career Flora Robson appeared in sixty films and more than one-hundred plays. She worked with many great actors, Lawrence Olivier, John Gielgud, Michael Redgrave and Richard Burton among them.

Flora Robson was not spoiled by her fame and was always a kindly lady. She never married and expressed deep regret at having no children. She once said, 'I've known very little personal love but the public has always shown me great affection.' There was nothing of the temperamental, difficult leading lady in Flora, and outside work she was very sympathetic to the plight of others. Her biographer recounts her many unpublicised acts of generosity in support of young aspiring actors, as in the case of the young South African, Leonard Dixon. She twice went on tour of South Africa, in 1960 with *The Aspern Papers* and again in 1962 with *The Corn is Green*, and, appalled by apartheid, insisted on performing to all-black audiences as well as white. She could not bear racism of any kind and although many were very surprised when Paul Robeson appeared in person during the episode of *This Is Your Life*, dedicated to Flora (in February 1961) he was there to thank her for what she had done to help him have his passport restored by the American government in 1957.

In later life, Flora retired to live quietly with her two sisters, Margaret and Sheila, in Wykeham Terrace, Brighton. She died, aged eighty-two, in Brighton Hospital after a short illness. She is buried in St Nicholas churchyard in Brighton.

Katherine Githa Sowerby (1876-1970)

Author and Playwright

Githa Sowerby spent the first thirty-six years of her life subject to the mercurial will of her father. In 1912 she transposed her story of domestic tyranny into a powerful blockbuster of a drama, *Rutherford and Son*, which was a sensational success in London and New York. For a few years she was lionised by society, acclaimed a ground breaking feminist writer with the dramatic powers of Ibsen, only to vanish into obscurity for nearly one hundred years.

Githa was born into a wealthy dynasty of glassmakers in Gateshead, owners of the Sowerby Ellison Glass Works, the leading makers of pressed glass in Europe and makers of superb stained glass and art glass. Her domineering grandfather, John Sowerby (1808- 1879), powered the business to its zenith and opened the much larger Ellison glass works in 1852. There were soon offices in London, Paris and Hamburg. Githa's father was John George Sowerby, born in 1849. As the eldest son, he had little choice but to enter the glassworks in 1871. At first he was happy enough. After his marriage in 1872, the six Sowerby children were born over a period of ten years. The eldest, John Lawrence, was the only son, and Githa was the second of five girls. The family lived in a luxurious house, *Ravenshill*, in Low Fell, Gateshead, where they employed seven resident servants. Githa grew to be a very intelligent and beautiful auburn-haired girl and although it brought her no joy she became her father's favourite. Because of this, Githa, alone of all the children, was

A stylised version of a portrait of Githa Sowerby
by George Percy Jacomb-Hood, circa 1912.

expected to sit with her parents' guests at dinner parties to entertain them. She actively disliked this, but later said how much she learnt about the technicalities of glass making, local employment issues and family business practices.

Githa remembered her childhood as bleak and unhappy and her mother as stern. She was disliked by their governesses because she was so lively and mischievous. True to middle class Victorian convention, John Lawrence was educated at Winchester College, while the five girls languished at home in the charge of indifferent governesses. Githa resented the girls' lack of formal education and, as events unfolded, her criticism of the convention that left girls economically dependent on men became very pertinent.

Her father's interest in the glassworks quickly waned, he lacked business acumen and his real interest was art. By 1883 the company was struggling and he was driven to resign both as Chairman and from the Board itself. This loss of income led him to be declared bankrupt and he had to sell the family home pay his debts. Gradually he relinquished all his involvement in the glass works and by 1896 had sold his complete portfolio of shares to pursue his love of painting. He moved the family every four or five years to ever-smaller houses to pay his debts or simply to give variety to the landscapes he could paint. In 1903, he was again declared bankrupt and could no longer support his family. When he died in 1914, John George Sowerby had spent several fortunes including his wife's. His estate was valued at £79 and his widow was left destitute.

Whilst Githa was appalled by her father's behaviour, she also saw his second bankruptcy in 1903 as a chance to break away. She set up house in London with her younger sister Millicent. They intended to earn their own livings by writing and illustrating children's books. Githa had previously been working as an author and had some poems published in magazines. Millicent was a largely self-taught but brilliant illustrator. In 1906 Marjorie, their disabled sister, joined their struggling household. It was at this time that Githa began to attend Fabian Society meetings regularly. Having seen the impact of capitalism on the poor and the rich, she had become a socialist.

In 1906 the Sowerby sisters' first book, *The Wise Book* was published and was quickly followed by *Childhood* and *The Bumbletoes*. All three sold well at home and abroad. Between 1906 and 1923 Githa published eleven successful children's books that her sister illustrated. She also wrote poetry and song lyrics. However, it is chiefly as a playwright that Katherine Githa Sowerby should be remembered.

In 1912 her first play, *Rutherford and Son,* was staged in London and was an absolute sensation. A devastating attack on the unacceptable face of capitalism, exposing the oppressive patriarchal system of the industrial North, it gripped audiences in the West End, on Broadway and across the world. There were 133 performances in London and 63 in New York, it was also produced in Australia and Canada, and was translated into five European languages. At the centre of the play are two horrific inventions, the personification of capitalism the 'Moloch,' to whom human sacrifices have to be made, and the equally hard tyrannical master of both his family and his glassworks, Rutherford, who attacks, degrades and rejects each of his children in turn. To his daughter Jane, banishment is a release and she condemns her father and his values. Githa had woven, from her own family history and her experiences of Tyneside, a brilliant morality play about domestic tyranny and class distinction. The play was published under the name K. G. Sowerby, but when it was discovered that it had been written by a woman, Githa became an overnight celebrity and a feminist hero. Her biographer, Katherine Riley, asserts that if the critics had known from the outset it was written by a woman it might never have been performed never mind rapturously received.

Githa found personal happiness that same year when she married Captain John Kaye Kendall, later widely known as Dum-Dum, the writer of light verse for *Punch* magazine. This was the most momentous time of her life, she was thirty-six, had achieved extraordinary success with her first play, was happily married and fully accepted as part of London Society, all of which she relished.

Githa continued to write plays with enthusiasm, believing that she could use the medium of theatre to make people question the way society functions. She felt strongly that social change was imperative and should begin with individuals because the power structures within the middle class family reflected the power structures in wider society.

In total Githa wrote four full-length plays apart from *Rutherford and Son,* but in her lifetime only one other was published, *Sheila,* which was performed nineteen times. Despite the fact that her plays were well received she quickly fell into obscurity.

Undoubtedly sexism in the theatre and in society played a part, after all people believed that women simply did not write plays. Aphra Benn was long dead! But there were no doubt other factors at work. Her plays challenge the status quo and were intellectually and socially provocative. She was personally very shy of publicity, and spurned interviews rather than encouraging them. She wrote independently and was never part of any feminist groups and so lacked a support network. She was fortunate in the timing of her first work, coming as it did at a time of great unrest (1910-1914), when Trade Union membership quadrupled, suffragists were militant and women wanted to be treated as equal to men. Unfortunately the timing of her other plays was positively unhelpful, the outbreak of the First World War put an end to any hope of staging *A Man and Some Women* and as the British Theatre was still unsubsidised commercial syndicates saw *The Stepmother* as too risky a project and it was only performed once

While Githa's career as a playwright stalled, her personal and social life took two unexpected turns. At the age of forty-one, she gave birth to a daughter, Githa Joan Peard Kendall. Joan thrived and became Mrs Smith, producing two grandsons for Githa. The second twist of fate was that May Buzzard, Githa's closest friend, died in 1922, and left a large and prestigious house, 18 Kensington Square, and her estate worth £44,000 to Githa. This windfall changed Githa's life, which had been a financial struggle for the last twenty years. Now there was no need to worry about money at all. Perhaps partly because of her changed circumstances, but already somewhat discouraged, Githa stopped writing and apart from one recently discovered play, never wrote again. Her compensation was that her personal life was so full. She spent as much time with her grandsons as she could, and she and John were very happy together until his tragic accidental death at a level crossing in 1952.

Undoubtedly hurt by the poor response to her work as a dramatist, a few months before her death Githa destroyed all her letters and photographs, saying that no one would be interested in them. She died peacefully at ninety-two, unreported in the press and certainly there was no obituary in *The Times*. It was as if her achievements had never been. The family added a tribute to her on her husband's commemorative plaque in St Brevita Church, Lanlivery, Cornwall. It reads simply, Katherine Githa, Author and Dramatist.

Fortunately this is not the end of the story. Githa Sowerby is beginning to enjoy something of a renaissance. *Rutherford and Son* was revived in 1980 and there have been several productions including one at the Royal National Theatre in 1994, by Northern Stage in 2009 and most recently by Northern Broadsides, in 2013. *The Stepmother* was performed at The Orange Tree in Richmond in 2013 and at Chichester in 2017. A biography of Sowerby, *'Looking for Githa'* by Patricia Riley was published in 2009. Sowerby's papers have all been donated to the Tyne and Wear Archives, and a blue plaque has finally been placed at her childhood home in Gateshead. The other memorial to Githa is the beautiful George Percy Jacob-Hood portrait, commissioned by her father in 1912, which perfectly captures the beauty and the spirit of this talented and formidable woman.

Nancy Spain
introducing Marlene
Dietrich at the Cafe de
Paris.

Nancy Brooker Spain (1917-1964)

Prominent Journalist and Broadcaster

Nancy Spain was a cub sports reporter for the *Newcastle Journal* who rose to become a national media celebrity and the real First Lady of Fleet Street before her tragic death in a plane crash.

Nancy was born at 1 Archbold Terrace, Jesmond and lived there for the next twenty-four years. She was the second and youngest daughter of Lieutenant–Colonel George Spain, a freeman of the City of Newcastle, a land agent and occasional broadcaster. Her mother, Norah Smiles, was granddaughter of Samuel Smiles the Victorian philanthropist, and the great niece of Mrs Isabelle Beeton.

Nancy recounted that as a child she learnt to ride on the Town Moor at five shillings an hour, 'with other little bourgeois tots.' From 1931-1934 she was educated at the prestigious girl's school Roedean, in Sussex, which she hated and later lampooned in a series of detective novels. While at Roedean she began wearing mannish clothes and developed the cut-glass speaking voice that was to serve her so well. On finishing school, Nancy became a cub sports reporter for the *Newcastle Journal* and simultaneously gained some acting experience in BBC radio plays recorded in the Bridge Street studios. She played lacrosse for Northumberland and Durham and hockey for the North of England team. Her summer sports were tennis and cricket and she was a member of Portland Park Tennis Club in Jesmond. When war broke out, Nancy joined the WRNS on Tyneside as a driver before being commissioned and sent to work in the WRNS press office in London. Her first book, the autobiographical *Thank you Nelson* (1945), became a best seller and marked the beginning of highly successful light literary career.

After the war, Nancy stayed in London and quickly became a media celebrity. Between 1945-54 she wrote a popular series of light hearted, camp detective novels. These included *Poison for the Teacher*, set in a girls' school on the Sussex coast called Radcliff Hall (a play on the name Radclyffe Hall, the author of the first explicitly lesbian novel, *Well of Loneliness* (1928)) and *Cinderella goes to the Morgue*, set in Newcastle, with a plot that revolves around a pantomime at the Theatre Royal. She also wrote a biography of Mrs Beeton and several more books of memoirs. On the back of her literary work, Nancy became a columnist for the *Daily Express*, *She* magazine and later the *News of the World*. Her writing style has been described as chatty, scatty, sporty and shot through with a mix of common sense and laugh-out-loud moments. She had a huge following. Nancy became something of a celebrity interviewer and was much given to copious references to her celebrity friends, including Marlene Dietrich, Hermione Gingold, Lena Horne and Noel Coward. She continued to make radio broadcasts and was very popular on *Woman's Hour*, she was a long serving panellist on the literary quiz, *My Word*, with Denis Norden and Frank Muir. In the 50s she became one of the best-known television celebrities of the time. She was good value for money, partly because of her ready wit, her fluency and her mischievous personality but also because of her appearance. An attractive woman, her distinctively male style of dress; trousers, monogrammed shirts and baggy jumpers, which at best could be described as chic butch, was in sharp contrast to the refined feminine and formal dress of her fellow panellists such as Lady Isobel Barnett. She was a great hit on television panel games such as *Juke Box Jury* and *What's My Line?* and a close friend of Gilbert Harding.

Rose Collis, Nancy Spain's biographer, wrote that Nancy was – a sort of not in though not exactly explicitly out, homosexual. It was widely known that while working in Newcastle she had a love affair with local sportswoman, Winifred Sargeant. Her friends were not surprised when, in 1950, she and her partner, Joan Ann Werner Laurie, who was the founder editor of *She* magazine, set up an unconventional household together. It consisted of Joan's son Nicholas, a younger boy Thomas, apparently Nancy's son from a relationship with Philip Youngman Carter, (husband of the crime writer Marjorie Allingham) and Sheila Van Damm, manager of the Windmill Theatre and rally driver. Nancy and Joan were known to be lesbians and were regulars at the Gateways club in Chelsea. It was in 1962 at London's Marquee club that Nancy performed and recorded *The Blaydon Races*, later published on the album, R&B from the Marquee.

Nancy had been commissioned to cover the Grand National in March 1964 and she and Joan were travelling there in a Piper Apache plane when it crashed just outside Aintree racecourse killing all four people on board. The Civil Aviation Accident Report concluded that, 'passenger interference cannot be ruled out.' Joan was learning to fly at the time. Nancy and Joan were cremated at Golders Green Crematorium in London and Nancy's ashes were placed in the family grave at Horsley in Northumberland.

When Nancy Spain died aged forty-seven, she was at the height of her career, the most famous female all-media celebrity of the day and an exceptional woman. On hearing of her death, Noel Coward wrote 'It is cruel that all that gaiety, intelligence and vitality should be snuffed out when so many bores and horrors are left living'.

Dame Irene Ward (1895-1980)

The 'Mother of the House'

Irene Ward was the longest serving woman MP to represent a North Eastern constituency. She achieved almost thirty-eight years in the House of Commons and became eventually - and affectionately - known as the 'Mother of the House'. Over the years she made her name as a feisty, assiduous and independent-minded back-bencher, just as prepared to challenge her own government as to criticise the opposition - especially if she felt she needed to do so to promote the interests of the people of her constituency and of her beloved North East. Despite - or perhaps because of - being a thorn in the side of governments over many years, she was made a Dame Commander (DBE) in 1955 and a Companion of Honour in 1975. She also had the distinction of getting four Private members bills on to the statute book - a record for a woman MP even today. Interestingly too, given how much publicity is given these days to Prime Ministers Questions (PMQs) in the House of Commons, is that Irene Ward was the first woman to ask a PMQ.

Irene Mary Bewick Ward spent her childhood on Tyneside with her widowed mother, who had moved back to the family's home region from London. She attended the Church High School in Jesmond, paid for by her father's relatives, and on leaving took up a variety of posts, both voluntary and

Irene Ward in 1968.

paid, eventually in 1921 becoming Secretary to a local coal owner. This post aroused her interest in North East industry and employment issues and her employer, Sir Cecil Cochran (a former Liberal MP), encouraged her to become active politically.

Her first attempt at Parliament was in 1924 at the age of twenty-nine. Although she was a candidate she could not vote herself as she was - just - under the age of thirty, which was then the qualifying age for women voters. She stood for the Conservative Party in Morpeth against well-known local miner Robert Smillie. By all accounts it was an extraordinarily stormy political initiation. The 'girl with a pretty face' as she was dubbed by the Press encountered strong hostility from the mining population of the constituency with threats to 'throw her out of the window' at one public meeting and a mass walk-out by miners at another. Challenged to go down a pit, she accepted, but that experience was made more than usually scary as orchestrated noises of falling coal and banging of machinery accompanied her visit. Her determination to engage with mining communities eventually commanded respect despite her political affiliation. The respect was mutual as Irene, from then on, was prepared to speak up for better conditions for miners and would urge coal owners to engage with miners and provide them with proper, detailed information about their industry. Even as early as 1924 she complained that although a Tory herself she felt that because no leading Tory politician at the time represented a constituency 'north of the Trent' that the problems of the North East region were being ignored.

Not surprisingly Irene came nowhere near winning in Morpeth in 1924 and suffered a similar defeat there in 1929, this time inflicted by prominent miners' leader, Ebenezer 'Ebby' Edwards.

Another seemingly hopeless cause beckoned when she was adopted as Conservative Candidate in Wallsend to fight the redoubtable Margaret Bondfield, the first woman Cabinet Minister. However by the time the 1931 election was called, Labour was deeply unpopular because of its divisions and because of high levels of unemployment and the economic slump. While having huge personal respect for her opponent, Irene threw herself into the campaign and, helped by the national anti-Labour swing, triumphed with a majority of over 7,000. She would defeat the same opponent again in 1935, although by a slimmer margin.

An independent streak was already apparent in Irene's maiden speech in May 1932 when she spoke of the need to improve miners' conditions and address the economic issues of the North East. She quickly became one of the most visible back benchers, speaking frequently in debates and even encountering the disapproval of the Speaker for 'flinging questions at Ministers'.

While always determined to bring constituency interests to the attention of the House from the outset of her Parliamentary career, Irene also took up wider causes. She was an early supporter of equal pay and she worked with other women MPs on a cross party basis on that issue and on a fairer deal for women regarding pensions and on their rights when marriages failed. Within the Conservative party she was active in seeking to get more women selected as candidates.

Internationally she was a strong supporter of the League of Nations and took part in a number of European and international Parliamentary activities. A memorable moment occurred during a visit to Germany in the 1930s after the Nazis had assumed power. During a reception for visiting Parliamentarians Irene's clear voice was suddenly heard above the hubbub saying to Germany's Foreign Minister 'You are talking rot Herr von Ribbentrop'!

During the Second World War she was keen to see women play a full part in the war effort. She chaired the all-party backbench committee that urged the Government to recognise and promote women's involvement. She was also a member of the women's consultative committee to the Ministry of Labour and served on the Select Committee overseeing public expenditure for the fighting forces - a Committee where secrecy and confidentiality had to be paramount.

Irene was a strong supporter of FANY, the First Aid Nursing Yeomanry. Her interest in this perhaps partly derived from her own service as a Voluntary Aid Detachment nurse during the First World War and through her friendship with fellow Northumbrian, Mary Baxter Ellis, who was Commandant of FANY from 1932 onwards. The name First Aid Nursing Yeomanry while indicative of some aspects of FANY's work does not describe the full range of activities that members undertook, particularly those who were involved in the highly dangerous and secret undercover operations in France. Many FANY members were outstandingly brave heroines, none more so perhaps than Violette Szabo, whom Irene knew personally. Irene cried when Szabo met her end in the Ravensbruck concentration camp and wrote a foreword to the subsequent book *Carve her Name with Pride* which immortalised her memory. Irene also wrote her own account of the work of the FANY members entitled *FANY Invicta*, published in 1954.

In the 1945 election Irene, not surprisingly given Labour's landslide victory, lost her Wallsend seat but returned to Parliament five years later, after winning another all-woman contest, this time against sitting Labour MP, Grace Colman in the neighbouring seat in Tynemouth. By then aged fifty-five, Irene had lost none of her energy or her enthusiasm for the political arena. Indeed her already long experience of Parliament seems to have emboldened her to speak out even more fearlessly when she felt the need to do so.

Examples of her opposing her own government include her criticism of the government's budget in 1956 and voting against her government in 1961 on the issue of hardship faced by fixed income groups.

She continued to be an active supporter of equal pay, and in 1952, along with

Labour MP Edith Summerskill, she took part in a demonstration organised by the Fawcett society where the two women MPs were driven in an open carriage to highlight the failure to address this issue properly.

North East concerns also continued to exercise her. She expressed alarm at the failure of the government to support the port of Tyne, which she felt was losing out to other ports around the country. She was also furious at the decision to move the northern headquarters of British Rail from Newcastle - the home of George Stephenson - to York.

She seems to have become increasingly frustrated at what she felt strongly was the North East's lack of political clout in government. Although a Minister for the North was created by Labour in the 1960s, Irene lost no time in pointing out that this Minister was largely silent in Parliament since the North East did not have its own Question Time in Parliament in the same way as Scotland and Wales.

Irene Ward enjoyed the record for the number of Private Members Bills an individual MP has succeeded in getting onto the statute book and still holds that record for those successfully introduced by a woman. During her career she brought forward four bills. The first, in 1938, was the Poor Law Amendment Bill, which introduced a weekly allowance for inmates in Poor Law Institutions who were otherwise destitute. The second, in 1954, was the Rights of Entry, Gas and Electricity Boards Bill which prevented gas and electricity officials entering a property without the occupier's consent. The third was the Nurses Amendment Act (1961), which ensured that all nurses and auxiliary nurses were properly registered. The fourth, in 1962, updated the 1872 Act on drunkenness.

Her frustration with the difficulty of getting the North East's case heard led her to stage two demonstrations on the floor of the House of Commons, demonstrations that not only drew considerable media attention but also cemented her reputation as a House of Commons character and fearless backbencher. In 1960 she sat, highly visible, on the front bench right next to the Prime Minister thus drawing media and public attention to herself in order to highlight the problems of unemployment on Tyneside.

The second occasion was in 1968. Irene was furious at the lack of time being given to backbenchers in a debate where she felt she was being denied the proper opportunity of speaking on behalf of her constituents. Her friend and fellow local MP, Bill Elliott, who was then a Tory whip, was asked to persuade her not to disrupt proceedings. He knew from the outset, however, that she was determined to make her point. Just before the vote was to be taken, she entered the Chamber in style, looking very smart and adorned with one of her signature hats. Again the Whips urged Bill Elliott to speak to her. Knowing the cause was hopeless he nonetheless approached her as requested but contented himself with saying gallantly 'In all the years I have known you I have never seen you look nicer' to which she responded 'Thank you dear'! She then left her seat and took up position in front of the Mace in defiance of the Speaker and Parliamentary procedure in order to prevent the result of the vote being announced. Refusing to resume her seat she shouted that she had been unable to protect the interests of her constituents and that Parliament 'had turned into a dictatorship'! Her point made, she was then escorted courteously but forcibly from the chamber by the ushers, having been named by the Speaker and incurring a temporary suspension.

Not content with demonstrating in the Commons, Irene had also caused a stir in the House of Lords on a previous occasion when she expostulated during a debate in annoyance at what was being said. By making her voice heard, she helped make history, since at the time there were no women members of the Upper House and no female voices were heard there.

Irene was also noted for outbursts of colourful language. Once, when infuriated at what she felt were evasive replies from Prime Minister Harold Wilson, she exclaimed 'I will poke the Prime Minister. I will poke him until I get a response!' Then, either unintentionally or possibly from a wicked and racy sense of humour - when annoyed that the need for new women's uniforms in the Royal Navy were not being given the same priority as those for men, intervened indignantly in the House of Commons to ask 'How long is the Minister going to hold up the skirts of the Wrens for the convenience of the sailors?'

Although a Conservative in Labour-dominated territory, she was friendly with Ellen Wilkinson and took opportunities to pay tribute publicly to her two-time opponent Margaret Bondfield. She made her mark both in Parliament and the North East and by the time she retired from the Commons in 1974, she had fulfilled the goals she had set herself when her first interest in politics was aroused so many years before. At the time of her retirement, she was the longest-serving woman MP and the oldest ever to be re-elected - records that were unbroken until very recently.

In 1974 she was elevated to the House of Lords with the title Baroness Ward of North Tyneside - an appropriate title since the North Tyneside borough included both of the constituencies she had represented, Wallsend and Tynemouth. She died in 1980 at the age of eighty-five.

Portrait by Sir F.W. Grant of
Louise Anne, Marchioness of
Waterford.

Lady Louisa Waterford (1818-1891)

Pre-Raphaelite Artist and Philanthropist

Louisa was born in 1818 in the magnificent Palais de Charost in the rue du Faubourg St. Honore in Paris. This building had formerly been the home of Pauline Borghese, Napoleon's sister and was acquired by the Duke of Wellington in 1814 in order to become the Residence of British Ambassadors to France. It still serves that purpose today. Louisa's father, Sir Charles Stuart (later the 1st Baron Stuart de Rothesay) had been appointed British Ambassador in 1815, a post he was to occupy until 1824 and then again from 1828 to 1830 - an extraordinary time to hold such a diplomatic position, in the immediate aftermath of Napoleon's final defeat at Waterloo.

Louisa's aristocratic family had some interesting connections. One of her great-grandmothers was Lady Mary Wortley Montagu and a great-grandfather was a co-founder of Kew Gardens. Louisa and her elder sister Charlotte seemed to have been given a good home education in which artistic pursuits played their part. At around age eleven - and with the ending of her father's term of office as Ambassador - Louisa with her family moved back to England to the family home at Highcliff Castle in Dorset, a house which needed to be rebuilt (because of coastal erosion) from 1831 to 1835 under the supervision of her father. The gardens of the house were magnificent and had been laid out by one of Northumberland's most famous sons, Capability Brown.

Louisa showed artistic talent from a young age and is recorded as occupying every spare moment in drawing and painting even when only six years old. She had little formal training but there was certainly encouragement from a governess who was keen that both she and her elder sister develop artistic skills. Louisa responded eagerly and indeed ever after throughout her life she was always accompanied by her sketch book.

As a young woman Louisa came into contact with members of the pre-Raphaelite group, in particular Dante Gabriel Rossetti, Holman Hunt and John Everett Millais. As well as having her artistic talent recognised by the group she also, as a beautiful young woman, was one of their sources of inspiration. She sat as a model for Millais and was described by Rossetti as 'a swell and a stunner!' According to her biographer Robert Franklin she was not tutored by Rossetti, as has been claimed, although he certainly rated her artistic talents highly but she was advised and monitored by John Ruskin over a period of some twenty years. Indeed it was Louisa who introduced the nine-year -old Rose la Touche to Ruskin (Rose's mother was a friend of Louisa) the young girl who Ruskin would fall in love with and would later want - unsuccessfully - to marry. As a young woman, too, Louisa had the opportunity to travel, finding particular artistic inspiration in her journeys through Italy.

These early contacts with the Pre-Raphaelites often lead Louisa to be described as a 'Pre-Raphaelite artist' but although she was undoubtedly influenced by them she is not easy to categorise. She also knew and admired Edwin Landseer and, having been able to travel through Italy as a young woman, she undoubtedly also found there much to influence her work and ideas.

In 1842 she married Henry de la Poer Beresford, 3rd Marquess of Waterford. He has been described as 'rather racy' and was thought of as wild yet, whether despite or because of this, or, more likely, through Louisa's calming influence on him which seems to have been considerable, the seventeen-year marriage proved to be a very happy one. After their marriage Henry and Louisa's main home was his family seat in Curraghmore, in County Waterford, Ireland. Once there, Louisa interested herself greatly in the running of the estate and the welfare of its staff, starting a school in a wing of their house, helping to set up a clothing factory and succeeding in establishing two new churches in the vicinity. In both churches she designed windows and in the one at Guilgach worked on the stained and painted glass.

However she and Henry also spent time travelling. Most autumns found them in Northumberland as Henry had inherited Ford Castle and estate from his grandmother, who had married into the Delaval family and where Louisa seems to have delighted in the Northumbrian countryside. They also journeyed together in continental Europe and spent time in London where Louisa pursued her interest in art and maintained personal contact with Ruskin and other leading lights in the art and cultural worlds.

In 1858, Louisa embarked on another tour of Italy with her sister Charlotte and it was there that she produced some of her most highly prized work, many examples of which are to be found in the Victoria and Albert museum today.

Tragically her husband, Henry, died the following year - in 1859 - in a riding accident, leaving Louisa a widow at a comparatively young age. Inheriting Ford from her husband it was there that she decided to live and she made it her home for the next thirty-two years.

She devoted herself single-mindedly to Ford, redesigning the village in order to provide better housing and a healthier environment. She provided a nurse for the community to help treat the sick, as well as visiting elderly and unwell villagers regularly herself. Keen to see that the children of the village received an education she founded the village school which in its heyday had more than 130 pupils. The school continued in existence until 1957 when the building became the village hall, renamed appropriately Lady Waterford Hall.

It is in the village school, over a period of over twenty years (from the 1860s to the 1880s) that Louisa accomplished her biggest and best known artistic work. This was a large series of biblical scenes in watercolour that adorn the walls of the school. Louisa's religion was very important to her and therefore it is not surprising that scenes from the bible would have been chosen by her. What adds special interest however is that many of the biblical characters portrayed are likenesses of the villagers themselves, including the children. They have been lovingly - and touchingly - depicted and, in addition to the artistic merit of the work it is a fascinating record of Ford and its people in the Victorian age. Michael Joicey's book Louisa *Anne, Marchioness of Waterford* contains details of the villagers depicted which included a fisherman, a blacksmith, her housekeeper, a butcher, a slater, a teacher, a mason, a miner and a publican. The children she so beautifully portrayed were the sons and daughters of such local people and some of their descendants still live in the vicinity of Ford today. Even the animals, birds and plants depicted often have a Northumbrian character including biblical shepherds with flocks of Cheviot sheep!

The great quality of Louisa's murals and the astounding achievement that they represented attracted huge interest at the time and people travelled to Ford from far and wide to admire them. The eminent painter - and Louisa's friend - G.F. Watts thought the school paintings were Louisa's best work and they influenced his own celebrated fresco in London's Lincoln's Inn.

Up until 1870 Louisa's other paintings had received little attention and had not been exhibited. Indeed there is some evidence that she had found this lack of interest upsetting, saying in a letter to her friend Eleanor Boyle 'poor humanity needs encouragement or one becomes too listless'! After 1870 or so - and combined with the impact of the school paintings - her work became better known. In 1890 she was invited to take her portfolio to Osborne House where her near contemporary, and friend, Queen Victoria, accepted as a gift one of her watercolours.

Louisa's religious and political views changed over time. From the high church beliefs of her youth she became more evangelical and appreciated the Presbyterian simplicity of the religion of many of the villagers of Ford and of its estate workers. She also changed politically. From the Conservative-supporting aristocratic circle in which she grew up she became increasingly Liberal in her outlook. She was close to Liberal Prime Minister Gladstone and counted him and his wife as dear friends. Her views are rather amusingly described by her friend Lady Paget who is recorded as saying: 'She is a frantic Gladstonian but hides it under a bushel because she naively confesses she never meets anyone in the society she frequents who sympathises with her.'

After the death of her mother in 1867 Louisa had responsibility for running not only Ford but also Highcliff Castle, the family home. She spent summers there and often entertained there, but - because it was not part of a community and village like Ford - had less social engagement there and missed the contact with villagers and local people which had become so precious to her. She did apply herself to some of the problems of the land there, however, which was prone to erosion and landslips. She tackled this challenge by the laying down of limestone and porphyry granite slabs to deflect the course of the 'Run' - the river outflow from Christchurch harbour. Even as late as the 1930s some of these flood control blocks were still in place.

In Victorian times famous artists were usually men who devoted themselves full time to their work. Their works often commanded high prices in commercial sales amidst much publicity whereas few of Louisa's works were sold, and then usually for charity. As a woman and an aristocrat occupying a Chatelaine-style role in running and managing two estates, it is perhaps not surprising that her achievements as an important artist often seem to be overshadowed and overlooked. She is often described as a 'gifted amateur' but this description for many does not do her full justice. G.F. Watts was a particular admirer of her art and said that he believed she was born an artist greater than any England has produced, the circumstances of her life alone preventing her from working on to the full achievement. Amusingly too, when her work was exhibited in the Dudley Gallery in 1883 - and attributed in a catalogue mistakenly to 'Mr. L Waterford' a critic exclaimed 'Who is Mr. Waterford, this new genius, reviving the glories of the Venetian school?'

Louisa died in 1891 aged seventy-three and is buried at Ford in a grave designed by G.F. Watts and his wife Mary Seton Watts. Her funeral testified to the affection of local people towards her and the great contribution she had made to life in Ford and Northumberland. Today Lady Waterford Hall and her paintings remain an important tourist attraction. Besides the decorated walls of the building the hall also contains some of her smaller artworks and examples of her sketchbooks. Watercolours by her are also in the possession of both the Victoria and Albert Museum and the National Portrait Gallery in London. In addition some fifty of her paintings are to be found displayed in Kiplin Hall in North Yorkshire - the owner of Kiplin Hall having been a relation of Louisa's by marriage.

The best known portrait of Louisa is that painted by Sir Francis Grant in 1859-60. There is also a terracotta statue of her by Boehm - a bronze cast of which is in the possession of Woburn Abbey. Sadly - as it would have doubtless provided valuable information for researchers into her life - much of Louisa's correspondence was destroyed. A recent biography of her by Robert Franklin appeared in 2011.

Biblical scenes by Lady Louisa Waterford at Ford School - now Lady Waterford Hall.

Ellen Wilkinson
addressing a huge meeting
in Trafalgar Square on
July 11 1937.

Ellen Wilkinson (1891-1947)

Cabinet Minister and Jarrow 'Crusader'

'Red Ellen', the 'Fiery Atom', the 'Pocket Pasionaria', 'Elfin Fury' and 'Little Miss Perky' were just some of the epithets given to Ellen Wilkinson during her political career. To earn that many nicknames she must have stood out from her colleagues - not surprisingly since she was one of only four women elected to Parliament in 1924 and was that Parliament's youngest MP. Over the next twenty years and more she played a prominent part in British political life and was both an outstanding Parliamentarian and an able Government Minister.

While Ellen is most remembered now for being the Member of Parliament for Jarrow at the time of the Jarrow March in the dark days of the 1930s, her links with the North East go back further, to her first days in Parliament when she was elected as MP for Middlesbrough East, which she represented for seven momentous years. Indeed the North East is key to an appreciation of her life's work.

Ellen was born in Ardwick, Manchester in 1891 and grew up in a working-class household where life was tough but not poverty stricken. Her home life was happy and she was close to both her parents, her two brothers and her elder sister, Annie. Her father, whose influence on her was very considerable, was a staunch Methodist and chapel was an important part of his life and that of his children. Ellen always retained a great affection for Methodism, remembering the hearty singing, the cheerful services, and the warmth and friendliness of the congregation in Grosvenor Street, Ardwick, which as a child she was very much part of.

She was a bright, intelligent child and her family encouraged her to learn and to be educated. In those days it was highly unusual for someone of Ellen's background to stay at school beyond fourteen, never mind attend University, but Ellen, by winning scholarships, eventually gained a place at Manchester University in 1910 to read history. She graduated in 1913. At University Ellen, who was already a member of the Independent Labour Party, was active in the Fabian Society and took part in many debates.

After obtaining her degree Ellen, who had originally considered a teaching career but decided that it did not suit her, worked for a time in Manchester as an organiser for the National Union of Women's Suffrage Societies. Then in 1915 she took up a post with the Trade Union movement and became the first woman to be appointed as an officer by her union, AUCE, later to become the National Union of Distributive and Allied Workers (NUDAW). The campaigns she was most associated with during that time aimed at recruiting women members, getting better pay for women workers and seeking to ensure that Trade Boards (which had been set up in 1909) delivered improved wage levels and working conditions.

Political activity went hand-in-hand with her trade unionism and Ellen was one of the many ILP members who also helped found the Communist Party of Great Britain, sharing in the initial enthusiasm of many on the British left for the Russian Revolution and the founding of the Soviet State. However, the increasingly hard-line and centralist aspects of Communism eventually alienated her and she resigned. In 1923 she was elected to Manchester City Council, winning the ward of Gorton South for Labour. Her local government experience was short-lived as her Union was keen to sponsor her for a Parliamentary seat and a year later she was elected at the 1924 general election as Labour MP for Middlesborough East.

'What a town to have the privilege of fighting' was Ellen's view of Middlesbrough, referring to its important industries of steel, shipbuilding and chemical works. While her maiden speech highlighted discrimination against women and urged that women under thirty be given the vote in the same way as men, Ellen was also very clear that she represented all her constituents, that thousands of men in Middlesbrough were unemployed and she intended to stand up for them at every opportunity.

Ellen's impact on Parliament and the public was immediate. Only 4'9' tall, youthful, with flaming red hair, a commanding - even unforgettable - voice and a vivid green dress she was a sensation. She was quickly in demand throughout the country - speaking at rallies and marches and supporting

Top) Ellen Wilkinson in her office.
Above) At the Jarrow Crusade.

colleagues in their Parliamentary seats. In the general strike of 1926 she chaired the Women's Committee for Miners' Wives and Children and undertook an exhaustive American fundraising tour, raising the equivalent of several millions of pounds in today's currency.

Ellen was easily re-elected for Middlesbrough East in 1929, but Labour was denied an overall majority and its leader, Ramsay MacDonald, was to head a coalition government that eventually embarked on policies unacceptable to his own MPs. Ellen went into opposition along with the majority of Labour's members and subsequently in the debacle of the 1931 election she lost her seat as did most of her party colleagues.

At the beginning of the 1930s Ellen was occupied with events both at home and abroad. She headed a delegation to India, which led to her calling for Gandhi's unconditional release and on the British Government to negotiate with him; she was an early opponent of Hitler and the Nazis, being denounced by them as a 'red-haired agitator' - a charge to which she unhesitatingly pleaded guilty. She also supported the Spanish Republicans and the Italian anti-fascists in a number of practical ways. At home, following the 1929 stock market crash, she became even more concerned with unemployment and that concern, of course, greatly intensified after she was selected as Labour candidate for Jarrow, a town that by 1932 had eighty per cent male unemployment. She would later describe it as 'The town that was murdered'. Even before being elected as the town's MP, she was leading delegations to Government. As MP she was tireless in the town's defence and supported the Council's decision to organise a march to London and present a petition to Parliament with all the determination she could muster. The Jarrow March - the 'Crusade' - touched the hearts of people everywhere on its route, yet at the time was unsympathetically received by Government and even by the Labour Party. It did, however, imprint itself gradually and deeply upon the nation's consciousness, fundamentally changing attitudes and contributing to the post-war determination that never again should such economic hardship and distress be tolerated. Ellen's own role in the 'Crusade' was recognised when she was awarded the freedom of Jarrow with the touching citation that 'To You the Borough has been an object of special care'.

The coalition government in power in the Second World War saw Ellen attain Ministerial Office, first in the Ministry of Pensions and then in the Home Office, where she had responsibility for air raid shelters. She spent much time visiting the areas experiencing the worst of the bombing.

With the Labour victory of 1945 came promotion to the Cabinet when Prime Minister Attlee appointed Ellen Minister of Education. For Ellen the 1944 Education Act had been a great coalition government achievement and she was determined to build on it. She announced that the school leaving age would be raised to fifteen by 1947 and to sixteen soon thereafter. She won support for this move in Cabinet and defeated a later move to try to postpone it. She succeeded in bringing in free school milk and expanding the school meals programme during her short period in office.

Over the years Ellen had battled health problems, particularly bronchitis and asthma and in February 1947 she died after also contracting pneumonia. As she had been using various prescribed drugs for some time there was some comment surrounding the inquest into her death that she might have deliberately taken an overdose but the Coroner firmly rejected this - a view also endorsed by those close to Ellen who knew that her willingness to take medication was much more linked to her determination to keep working at all costs.

Ellen had many close friends during her life as well as romantic attachments. She was engaged once, at University, to Walton Newbold but broke the engagement off. Later she was also linked to John Jagger, the impressive President of NUDAW, and to Frank Horrabin, MP for Peterborough, although the exact nature of these relationships is not known and Ellen's personal correspondence was destroyed after her death. A relationship with Herbert Morrison, from the available evidence, seems highly likely according to Ellen's biographer, Betty Vernon, despite the fact that they were from different wings of the Labour Party. Ellen had supported Morrison through unsuccessful attempts to become Labour Leader and had also worked very closely with him in government over a number of years - yet Morrison failed to mention her at all in his autobiography, an extraordinary omission which, apparently, raised many eyebrows at the time.

In addition to her political career Ellen found time for writing. Among a number of works she produced a novel *Clash* in 1929 and some non-fiction including the entertaining *Peeps at Politicians* of 1931 where she profiles, with affection and humour, some of her fellow Parliamentarians from across the political spectrum.

Besides the Betty Vernon biography of Ellen there are a number of ways in which she is remembered. There is a plaque on the site of her house in Ardwick, Manchester; one of Tyne and Wear's rapid transit 'Metro' trains is named after her; there have been commemorative events about her in Parliament and recently she featured in the *My Hero* series on BBC Radio 4.

Wellcome

Dr Ethel Williams.

Dr Ethel Williams (1863-1948)

Newcastle's First Woman Doctor and Suffragist

At the beginning of the twentieth century, Dr Ethel Williams was arguably the best-known woman on Tyneside. As Newcastle's first woman doctor, the first woman to set up in general practice in the city, the first woman in the city to drive a motor car and a leading suffragist, she made a great impact.

Ethel was born in 1863 in Norfolk and studied medicine in London, where in 1891 she graduated from the London School of Medicine for Women. She then gained practical hospital experience in Paris and Vienna, as women were not permitted to train in British hospitals at the time.

She came to Newcastle in 1906 and set up her general medical practice alongside Dr Ethel Bentham. Their premises were first in Ellison Place and then in Osborne Terrace, Jesmond. Dr Bentham was a notable woman and, like Ethel Williams, a suffragist. She was also an early Labour supporter and after a few years in the North East ended up in London, for a time sharing a flat with Marion Phillips and eventually, at the age of sixty-eight, becoming MP for Islington East.

Ethel Williams, on the other hand, remained in the North East for the rest of her life and dedicated herself to the health and welfare of some of Tyneside's poorest women. She is rightly described as a social reformer as well as a doctor and her work in this respect was nationally as well as locally recognised, for example through her work as an investigator for the National Commission on the Poor Laws. In 1917 Ethel co-founded the Northern Women's Hospital (now the Nuffield Health Clinic) on Osborne Road. She was also one of the founding members of the Medical Women's Federation.

From all accounts, Ethel had a devoted following among her patients and this was true not just of those in the poorest areas but also in the more affluent parts of Newcastle such as Jesmond and Heaton where she was greatly respected for her skill and commitment.

Outside her medical work Ethel chaired the North East Society of Women's Suffrage. It is said that her car was very useful to them in their campaigning! She took part in many demonstrations calling for Women to be given the vote. Her colourful suffragist banner, now in the possession of Newcastle University Library's Special Collection, was carried in marches in London and the North East. The name of Newcastle upon Tyne at the top is accompanied by the three castles from the city's coat of arms against a vivid red background. The banner was probably paraded in the famous 'Mud March' of 1907 in London as well as in the impressive 1909 demonstration in Newcastle. Ethel was also a frequent public speaker at demonstrations and meetings and - despite her demanding medical duties - somehow found time to organise and campaign indefatigably for the suffrage movement over the whole of the period from 1905 onwards.

Politically Ethel was initially allied to the Liberal Party but became disappointed with what she saw as their lukewarm support for women's votes and turned increasingly to the Independent Labour Party. Her pacifist stance in the First World War confirmed this leftwards move. She also supported the Women's International League for Peace and freedom and, like Marion Phillips, wanted to see women given a role in the new international organisations being founded at the end of the conflict.

Ethel was a member and supporter of Newcastle's Literary and Philosophical Society and served as a Justice of the Peace.

She retired from medicine in 1924 at the age of sixty-one and her practice was taken over by another woman doctor, Dr Mona McNaughton. By that time, the number of women doctors in Newcastle had grown to fourteen. Ethel went to live in Stocksfield in the Tyne Valley in a house called *The Bramble Patch*. Her long-standing companion Frances Hardcastle, who was a notable mathematician and granddaughter of the astronomer Herschel, retired with her and they lived together there until 1941 when Frances died. Ethel died in 1948 aged eighty-five.

Ethel Williams' memory lives on in a number of ways and Newcastle University holds some of her records and papers. The University also named a Hall of Residence after her. Ethel Williams Hall in Benton was originally a residence for women only. In the 1990s most of the hall, other than the eighteenth century house at its core, was demolished and the site sold. However, the houses now occupying the site have retained the link with Ethel, being named Williams Park.

On July 18 2018 Ethel Williams was honoured by Newcastle City Council with the placing of a plaque on the house in Osborne Terrace, Jesmond, where she lived and where her surgery was situated.

Select Bibliography

Mary Astell *(Moira Kilkenny)*
Stanford Encyclopaedia of Philosophy, 2015
Mary Astell by Penelope Whitworth, includes excellent Bibliography
Oxford Dictionary of National Biography, Astell Mary (1666-1731) by Ruth Perry, 2004
The Celebrated Mary Astell: An Early English Feminist, Ruth Perry,
      University of Chicago Press, 1986
A Serious Proposal to the Ladies for the Advancement of their True and Greatest Interest Parts
      1 and 2, Mary Astell, 1694 and 1697
Some reflections on Marriage... , 1700, 1703, 1706 and 1730
Letters Concerning the Love of God, 1705 and 1730

Gertrude Bell *(Moira Kilkenny)*
The Extraordinary Gertrude Bell, edited by Mark Jackson and Andrew Parkin,
      Tyne Bridge Publishing, 2015
All Gertrude Bell's papers are held by Newcastle University
There is a permanent Gertrude Bell exhibition in Kirkleatham Museum in Redcar,
      Yorkshire.
Two films of her life have been made recently, *A documentary* (2016),
      Letters from Baghdad, and an American epic biography (2005), *Queen of the Desert*

Margaret Bondfield *(Joyce Quin)*
A Life's Work, Margaret Bondfield, 1948
Women on the March, John Sleight, 1986
Commemorative Booklet by North Tyneside Fabian Society

Mary Eleanor Bowes *(Moira Kilkenny)*
Bowes and Strathmores, Sunniside Local History Society
Wedlock, How Georgian Britain's Worst Husband Met His Match, Wendy Moore,
      Phoenix 2009

Elinor Brent-Dyer *(Moira Kilkenny)*
Information Sheets from Friends of the Chalet School, chaletschool.org.uk
Behind the Chalet School; A Biography of Elinor M Brent-Dyer by Helen McLelland,
      Bettany Press, 1996
The Chalet School Stories are still in print

Kathleen Brown *(Joyce Quin)*
Tyne and Wear Archives
Family information including from a letter from Donald Fraser supplied by Rona Willett
      and additional information from Rona Willett, Jean Fraser, Ann Moore, Charles
      Moore and Fred Hasson.

Josephine Butler *(Joyce Quin)*
Reminiscences of a Great Crusade, Josephine Butler, 1896
Josephine Butler, Jane Jordan, 2001
Leaflet published by Kirknewton Church

Ivy Lillian Close *(Moira Kilkenny)*
BBC News, 14 Jan 2017, rediscovery of Sir Arthur Hackett's Portrait of Ivy Close
Internet Movie Base (IMDb)
There are no publications. Preston Park Museum in Stockton on Tees holds a collection
    of documents relating to her.

Grace Colman *(Joyce Quin)*
John Sleight, *Women on the March*, 1986
Commemorative Booklet by North Tyneside Fabian Society
Tynemouth constituency election material from 1950

Ida and Louise Cook *(Moira Kilkenny)*
Safe Passage by Ida Cook, Harlequin Mira, 1976
Mary Burchell novels, (still available), Mills and Boon

Catherine Cookson (Joyce Quin)
Our Kate, Catherine Cookson, 1969
Catherine Cookson: A biography, Debbie Jabbour, 2012

Grace Darling *(Moira Kilkenny)*
Grace Darling Her True Story, Thomasina Darling, 1880
RNLI Grace Darling Museum, Bamburgh, Northumberland
Grace Darling, The Heroine of the Farne Islands, Christine Bell, Darling Books, 2004

Emily Davies *(Joyce Quin)*
Emily Davies and the Liberation of Women: 1830-1921, Daphne Bennett, 1990
Feminism and Quakerism in the Nineteenth Century, Article in Quaker Studies by
    Elizabeth A. O'Donnell.

Emily Wilding Davison *(Joyce Quin)*
Gertrude Colmore, Biography, 1913
The Life and Death of Emily Wilding Davison, Ann Morley and Liz Stanley, 1988
One Way Ticket to Epsom, John Sleight, 1988

Ruth Dodds *(Joyce Quin)*
Pilgrimage of Grace, Madeleine Dodds and Ruth Dodds, 1915
The Pitman's Pay - A Historical Play in four Acts, Ruth Dodds, 1923
Ruth Dodds' Diaries, Maureen Calcott, 1996

Elizabeth Elstob *(Moira Kilkenny)*
Men of Mark 'Twixt Tyne and Tweed, Richard Welford, vol.2, 1895
The Saxon Nymph Elizabeth Elstob
History Today, 4th Feb 2016 *The First Female Anglo-Saxonist*, Yvonne Seale
Women Medievalists and the Academy, (ed Jane Chance) Chapter 1. Elizabeth Elstob,
     S.F.D. Hughes

Lady Sybil Grey *(Moira Kilkenny)*
Lady Sybil: Empire, War and Revolution, Simon Boyd, Hayloft Publishing, 2017
The Forgotten Hospital, Michael Harmer, Springwood Books, 1982

Isa Jobling *(Moira Kilkenny)*
A Romance with the North East: Robert and Isa Jobling, John Millard,
     Tyne and Wear Museums, 1992
The Artists of Northumbria, Marshall Hall, Marshall Associates, 1982

Winifred Laver *(Moira Kilkenny)*
Gateshead's Sister Winifred and the Vine Street Mission, David Percy
A Tale of two Decades, William Hodgson, Leo Ormston, 2008

Dorothy Lawson *(Moira Kilkenny)*
Life of Mrs. Dorothy Lawson of St. Antony's near Newcastle-upon-Tyne in Northumberland,
     written in the early seventeenth century by her former chaplain, William Palmes,
     S.J.
Oxford Dictionary of National Biography, Lawson [née Constable], Dorothy,
     Claire Walker
Priest of the Plague, Henry Morse, P. Caraman, 1957.
Men of Mark 'Twixt Tyne and Tweed, Richard Welford. vol 3.1895

Connie Lewcock *(Joyce Quin)*
Information from her family and acquaintances
Connie Lewcock's unpublished autobiography
Online searches including Wikipedia

Charlotte Marsh *(Moira Kilkenny)*
To Make Their Mark: Women's Suffrage Movement in North East England, 1900-1914,
     David Neville, 1997
Oxford Dictionary of National Biography, Marsh, Charlotte Augusta Leopoldine,
     Michelle Myall
Votes for Women: Forgotten Suffragettes, Beverley Cook, Museum of London
     (As part of their Votes for Women Exhibition) 2018

Harriet Martineau *(Joyce Quin)*
Life in the Sick Room, Harriet Martineau, 1844
Harriet Martineau, Florence Fenwick Miller, 1884

Kate Maxey *(Moira Kilkenny)*
A Nurse at the Front: The First World War Diaries of Sister Edith Appleton, Ruth Cowen
Durham at War –Mapping the story of County Durham and its people in the
      First World War, Durham Record Office

Elizabeth Montagu *(Moira Kilkenny)*
Oxford Dictionary of National Biography, Montagu, Elizabeth, B.B. Schnorrenberg
Slipshod Sibyls: Rejection and the Woman Poet, Germain Greer, 1995

Mo Mowlam *(Joyce Quin)*
Mo Mowlam, Julia Langdon, 2000
Momentum, Mo Mowlam, 2002
Hansard (The Parliamentary Journal)
Personal reminiscences
Why deny Mo Mowlam, my Step-Mum, credit for the Good Friday Agreement?
      Henrietta Norton, Opinion piece, *The Guardian*, 12 April 2018

Dr Ruth Nicholson *(Moira Kilkenny)*
Angels of Mercy. A Women's Hospital on the Western Front 1914-18, Eileen Crofton,
      Birlinn Ltd, 2013
The Hospitals 1800-1948, Brian Abel-Smith, Heinnemann Educational Books Ltd, 1964
Durham Record Office, Medical Women's Federation Archive
The Preventive and Curative Treatment of Gas Gangrene by Mixed Serums,
      Frances Ivens .BMJ 1918.

Rachel Parsons *(Moira Kilkenny)*
Magnificent Women and their Revolutionary Machines, Henrietta Heald, Unbound, 2015
What was a girl to do? Rachel Parsons 1885-1956 engineer and feminist campaigner,
      Henrietta Heald, Blue Stocking, Unbound, 2014
Oxford Dictionary of National Biography, Parsons, Sir Charles Algernon,
      Anita McConnell

Marion Phillips *(Joyce Quin)*
Women at Westminster: An account of women in the British Parliament 1918-1966,
      Pamela Brookes, 1967
Women on the March, John Sleight, 1986

Mabel Philipson *(Joyce Quin)*
Women at Westminster: An account of women in the British Parliament 1918-1966, Pamela
      Brookes, 1967
Women on the March, John Sleight, 1986
Hansard, (The Parliamentary Journal)

Anna Richardson *(Joyce Quin)*
My bondage and my freedom, Frederick Douglass, 1855
Various newspaper and online articles including Wikipedia
Women in the Quaker Community: The Richardson Family of
      Newcastle upon Tyne c1815-60, Quaker Studies. Jonathan Mood

Muriel Robb *(Moira Kilkenny)*
A Little-known Wimbledon singles champion, Mark Ryan, tennisforum.com, 2010
Minute books of Jesmond Lawn Tennis Club
Muriel's second cousin, Anne Induni, has researched the family and helped with
    additional family information

Denise Robertson *(Joyce Quin)*
Agony? Don't get me started, Denise Robertson, 2006
The Belgate Trilogy: *The Beloved People; Strength for the Morning; Towards Jerusalem*,
    Denise Robertson, 1992-93
Remember the Moment, Denise Robertson, 1990
The Second Wife, Denise Robertson, 1995

Flora Robson *(Moira Kilkenny)*
Flora: An Appreciation of the Life and Work of Dame Flora Robson, Kenneth Barrow,
    Heinemann Ltd, 1981

Katherine Githa Sowerby *(Moira Kilkenny)*
Looking for Githa, Patricia Riley, New Writing North, 2009

Nancy Spain *(Moira Kilkenny)*
A Trouser-wearing Character: the life and times of Nancy Spain, Rose Collis, 1997

Irene Ward *(Joyce Quin)*
Women at Westminster: An account of women in the British Parliament 1918-1966,
    Pamela Brookes, 1967
Irene Ward, F.A.N.Y *Invicta*, 1955
Women on the March, John Sleight, 1986

Louisa Waterford *(Joyce Quin)*
Ford Village Hall commemorative booklet
Biography of Louisa Waterford, R. Franklin, 2011
Louisa Waterford and John Ruskin - For You have not Falsely Praised,
    Caroline Ing-Chambers, 2015
*Louisa Waterford: A Look at her Life and a guide to the murals painted by her at Ford,
    Northumberland,*Michael Joicey, 1993

Ellen Wilkinson *(Joyce Quin)*
Ellen Wilkinson 1891-1947, Betty Vernon, 1982.
Women on the March, John Sleight, 1986
Notes from commemorative event in House of Commons, 2015
Information from local people who knew her

Ethel Williams *(Joyce Quin)*
Wikipedia
Family information
To Make their Mark, David Neville, 1997

Acknowledgements

The authors wish to thank the following who provided valuable information, both written and oral, or who gave support in advising and proof-reading in the course of producing *Angels of the North*.

Dr Gordon Adam; Cynthia Barker and Janet Dugdale (daughter and granddaughter of Connie Lewcock); Lord Jeremy Beecham; Mr. Simon Boyd (grandson of Sybil Grey); John Brennan,; Jill Foster, Secretary, Jesmond Lawn Tennis Club; Maureen Hird (daughter of William Henry Cusack, loyal party worker and sometime agent for Ellen Wilkinson, MP); Anne Induni (second cousin of Muriel Robb); Ann Moore, Charles Moore, Charlotte Moore, Darien and Jean Fraser, Fred Hasson and Rona Willett (members of Kathleen Brown's family); Dr Peter Regan; the Ferens Gallery, Hull; the staff of TWAM (Tyne and Wear Archives and Museums); the staff of the Literary and Philosophical Library, Newcastle upon Tyne; Guy MacMullen; Michael Kilkenny and Rachel Kilkenny.

The authors would also like to give warm thanks to the staff of Tyne Bridge Publishing and in particular to David Hepworth, its Manager, for his work, advice, friendship and unfailing support in the preparation of this volume.